THE YALE SHAKESPEARE

Edited by

Wilbur L. Cross   Tucker Brooke

Published under the Direction
of the
Department of English, Yale University,
on the Fund
Given to the Yale University Press in 1917
by the Members of the
Kingsley Trust Association
(Scroll and Key Society of Yale College)
to Commemorate the Seventy-Fifth Anniversary
of the Founding of the Society

·: *The Yale Shakespeare* :·

VENUS AND ADONIS
LUCRECE
AND THE MINOR POEMS

EDITED BY
ALBERT FEUILLERAT

NEW HAVEN · YALE UNIVERSITY PRESS
LONDON · HUMPHREY MILFORD
OXFORD UNIVERSITY PRESS · MCMXXVII

TABLE OF CONTENTS

The facsimile opposite reproduces from a copy in the Yale Elizabethan Club the title-page of the rare second edition of 'Venus and Adonis.' Four copies of this edition are known to survive. (See p. 176.)

VENVS
AND ADONIS

Vilia miretur vulgus: mihi flauus Apollo
Pocula Castalia plena ministret aqua.

LONDON.

Imprinted by Richard Field, and are to be sold at
the signe of the white Greyhound in
Paules Church-yard.
1594.

Venus and Adonis

—

'Vilia miretur vulgus; mihi flavus Apollo
Pocula Castalia plena ministret aqua.'

TO THE RIGHT HONOURABLE HENRY WRIOTHESLEY,

EARL OF SOUTHAMPTON, AND BARON OF TICHFIELD.

RIGHT HONOURABLE,

I know not how I shall offend in dedicating my unpolished lines to your lordship, nor how the world will censure me for choosing so strong a prop to support so weak a burthen: only, if your honour seem 8 but pleased, I account myself highly praised, and vow to take advantage of all idle hours, till I have honoured you with some graver labour. But if the first heir of my invention prove deformed, I shall be 12 sorry it had so noble a godfather, and never after ear so barren a land, for fear it yield me still so bad a harvest. I leave it to your honourable survey, and your honour to your heart's content; which I wish 16 may always answer your own wish and the world's hopeful expectation.

Your honour's in all duty,

WILLIAM SHAKESPEARE.

—

EVEN as the sun with purple-colour'd face
Had ta'en his last leave of the weeping morn,
Rose-cheek'd Adonis hied him to the chase;

Epigraph; *cf. n.*
Ded. 2 Wriothesley; *cf. n.*   13 ear: *plough*
2 weeping: *shedding dew*   3 Rose-cheek'd; *cf. n.*   hied him: *hastened*

Hunting he lov'd, but love he laugh'd to scorn;　4
　　Sick-thoughted Venus makes amain unto him,
　　And like a bold-fac'd suitor 'gins to woo him.

'Thrice fairer than myself,' thus she began,
'The field's chief flower, sweet above compare,　8
Stain to all nymphs, more lovely than a man,
More white and red than doves or roses are;
　　Nature that made thee, with herself at strife,
　　Saith that the world hath ending with thy life.　12

'Vouchsafe, thou wonder, to alight thy steed,
And rein his proud head to the saddle-bow;
If thou wilt deign this favour, for thy meed
A thousand honey secrets shalt thou know:　16
　　Here come and sit, where never serpent hisses;
　　And being set, I'll smother thee with kisses:

'And yet not cloy thy lips with loath'd satiety,
But rather famish them amid their plenty,　20
Making them red and pale with fresh variety;
Ten kisses short as one, one long as twenty:
　　A summer's day will seem an hour but short,
　　Being wasted in such time-beguiling sport.'　24

With this she seizeth on his sweating palm,
The precedent of pith and livelihood,
And, trembling in her passion, calls it balm,
Earth's sovereign salve to do a goddess good:　28
　　Being so enrag'd, desire doth lend her force
　　Courageously to pluck him from his horse.

---

5 makes amain: *goes in haste*　　　　　　　　　　**9** Stain; *cf. n.*
11 Nature . . . strife; *cf. n.*　　　　**12** the world . . . life; *cf. n.*
18 set: *seated*　　　　　　　　　　　　　　　　　**24** wasted: *spent*
25 sweating palm; *cf. n.*　　　**26** precedent: *sign*　　livelihood: *vigor*

Over one arm the lusty courser's rein,
Under her other was the tender boy,   32
Who blush'd and pouted in a dull disdain,
With leaden appetite, unapt to toy;
    She red and hot as coals of glowing fire,
    He red for shame, but frosty in desire.   36

The studded bridle on a ragged bough
Nimbly she fastens;—O! how quick is love:—
The steed is stalled up, and even now
To tie the rider she begins to prove: 40
    Backward she push'd him, as she would be thrust,
    And govern'd him in strength, though not in lust.

So soon was she along, as he was down,
Each leaning on their elbows and their hips: 44
Now doth she stroke his cheek, now doth he frown,
And 'gins to chide, but soon she stops his lips;
    And kissing speaks, with lustful language broken,
    'If thou wilt chide, thy lips shall never open.' 48

He burns with bashful shame; she with her tears
Doth quench the maiden burning of his cheeks;
Then with her windy sighs and golden hairs
To fan and blow them dry again she seeks: 52
    He saith she is immodest, blames her miss;
    What follows more she murthers with a kiss.

Even as an empty eagle, sharp by fast,
Tires with her beak on feathers, flesh and bone,   56
Shaking her wings, devouring all in haste,
Till either gorge be stuff'd or prey be gone;
    Even so she kiss'd his brow, his cheek, his chin,
    And where she ends she doth anew begin.   60

37 ragged: *rough*
53 miss; *cf. n.*   55 empty: *hungry*   40 prove: *attempt*
56 Tires; *cf. n.*

Forc'd to content, but never to obey,
Panting he lies, and breatheth in her face;
She feedeth on the steam, as on a prey,
And calls it heavenly moisture, air of grace;   64
  Wishing her cheeks were gardens full of flowers,
    So they were dew'd with such distilling showers.

Look! how a bird lies tangled in a net,
So fasten'd in her arms Adonis lies;   68
Pure shame and aw'd resistance made him fret,
Which bred more beauty in his angry eyes:
  Rain added to a river that is rank
    Perforce will force it overflow the bank.   72

Still she entreats, and prettily entreats,
For to a pretty ear she tunes her tale;
Still is he sullen, still he lowers and frets,
'Twixt crimson shame and anger ashy-pale;   76
  Being red, she loves him best; and being white,
    Her best is better'd with a more delight.

Look how he can, she cannot choose but love;
And by her fair immortal hand she swears,   80
From his soft bosom never to remove,
Till he take truce with her contending tears,
  Which long have rain'd, making her cheeks all wet;
    And one sweet kiss shall pay this countless debt.   84

Upon this promise did he raise his chin
Like a dive-dapper peering through a wave,
Who, being look'd on, ducks as quickly in;
So offers he to give what she did crave;   88
  But when her lips were ready for his pay,
    He winks, and turns his lips another way.

61 content: *acquiesce; cf. n.*   71 rank; *cf. n.*   78 more: *greater*
82 *Cf. n.*   86 dive-dapper; *cf. n.*   90 winks: *shuts his eyes*

Never did passenger in summer's heat
More thirst for drink than she for this good turn. 92
Her help she sees, but help she cannot get;
She bathes in water, yet her fire must burn:
  'O! pity,' 'gan she cry, 'flint-hearted boy:
  'Tis but a kiss I beg; why art thou coy? 96

'I have been woo'd, as I entreat thee now,
Even by the stern and direful god of war,
Whose sinewy neck in battle ne'er did bow,
Who conquers where he comes in every jar; 100
  Yet hath he been my captive and my slave,
  And begg'd for that which thou unask'd shalt have.

'Over my altars hath he hung his lance,
His batter'd shield, his uncontrolled crest, 104
And for my sake hath learn'd to sport and dance,
To toy, to wanton, dally, smile, and jest;
  Scorning his churlish drum and ensign red,
  Making my arms his field, his tent my bed. 108

'Thus he that overrul'd I oversway'd,
Leading him prisoner in a red-rose chain:
Strong-temper'd steel his stronger strength obey'd,
Yet was he servile to my coy disdain. 112
  O, be not proud, nor brag not of thy might,
  For mastering her that foil'd the god of fight!

'Touch but my lips with those fair lips of thine,—
Though mine be not so fair, yet are they red,— 116
The kiss shall be thine own as well as mine:
What seest thou in the ground? hold up thy head:
  Look in mine eyeballs, there thy beauty lies;
  Then why not lips on lips, since eyes in eyes? 120

91 passenger: *traveler*   100 jar: *conflict*
104 uncontrolled; *cf. n.*   114 foil'd: *defeated*

'Art thou asham'd to kiss? then wink again,
And I will wink; so shall the day seem night;
Love keeps his revels where there are but twain;
Be bold to play, our sport is not in sight: 124
    These blue-vein'd violets whereon we lean
    Never can blab, nor know not what we mean.

'The tender spring upon thy tempting lip
Shows thee unripe, yet mayst thou well be tasted.   128
Make use of time, let not advantage slip;
Beauty within itself should not be wasted:
    Fair flowers that are not gather'd in their prime
    Rot and consume themselves in little time.   132

'Were I hard-favour'd, foul, or wrinkled-old,
Ill-nurtur'd, crooked, churlish, harsh in voice,
O'erworn, despised, rheumatic, and cold,
Thick-sighted, barren, lean, and lacking juice,   136
    Then mightst thou pause, for then I were not for
      thee;
    But having no defects, why dost abhor me?

'Thou canst not see one wrinkle in my brow;
Mine eyes are grey and bright, and quick in turn-
    ing;   140
My beauty as the spring doth yearly grow;
My flesh is soft and plump, my marrow burning;
    My smooth moist hand, were it with thy hand felt,
    Would in thy palm dissolve, or seem to melt.   144

'Bid me discourse, I will enchant thine ear,
Or like a fairy trip upon the green,
Or like a nymph, with long dishevell'd hair,

129-132 *Cf. n.*   130 *Cf. n.*
135 O'erworn: *worn out by time*   136 Thick-: *weak-*

Dance on the sands, and yet no footing seen: 148
    Love is a spirit all compact of fire,
    Not gross to sink, but light, and will aspire.

'Witness this primrose bank whereon I lie;
These forceless flowers like sturdy trees support
    me;   152
Two strengthless doves will draw me through the sky,
From morn till night, even where I list to sport me:
    Is love so light, sweet boy, and may it be
    That thou shouldst think it heavy unto thee?   156

'Is thine own heart to thine own face affected?
Can thy right hand seize love upon thy left?
Then woo thyself, be of thyself rejected,
Steal thine own freedom, and complain on theft.   160
    Narcissus so himself himself forsook,
    And died to kiss his shadow in the brook.

'Torches are made to light, jewels to wear,
Dainties to taste, fresh beauty for the use,   164
Herbs for their smell, and sappy plants to bear;
Things growing to themselves are growth's abuse:
    Seeds spring from seeds, and beauty breedeth
      beauty;
    Thou wast begot; to get it is thy duty.   168

'Upon the earth's increase why shouldst thou feed,
Unless the earth with thy increase be fed?
By law of nature thou art bound to breed,
That thine may live when thou thyself art dead;   172
    And so in spite of death thou dost survive,
    In that thy likeness still is left alive.'

148 footing: *footprint*   149 compact: *composed*
150 aspire: *ascend*   157 affected to: *in love with*
158 *Cf. n.*   161 Narcissus; *cf. n.*

By this the love-sick queen began to sweat,
For where they lay the shadow had forsook them,   176
And Titan, tired in the mid-day heat,
With burning eye did hotly overlook them;
  Wishing Adonis had his team to guide,
  So he were like him and by Venus' side.   180

And now Adonis with a lazy spright,
And with a heavy, dark, disliking eye,
His louring brows o'erwhelming his fair sight,
Like misty vapours when they blot the sky,   184
  Souring his cheeks, cries, 'Fie! no more of love:
  The sun doth burn my face; I must remove.'

'Ay me,' quoth Venus, 'young, and so unkind?
What bare excuses mak'st thou to be gone?   188
I'll sigh celestial breath, whose gentle wind
Shall cool the heat of this descending sun:
  I'll make a shadow for thee of my hairs;
  If they burn too, I'll quench them with my tears. 192

'The sun that shines from heaven shines but warm,
And lo! I lie between that sun and thee:
The heat I have from thence doth little harm,
Thine eye darts forth the fire that burneth me;   196
  And were I not immortal, life were done
  Between this heavenly and earthly sun.

'Art thou obdurate, flinty, hard as steel?
Nay, more than flint, for stone at rain relenteth. 200
Art thou a woman's son, and canst not feel
What 'tis to love? how want of love tormenteth?
  O, had thy mother borne so hard a mind,
  She had not brought forth thee, but died unkind. 204

177 Titan: *the sun*   197, 198 *Cf. n.*   200 relenteth: *softens*
203, 204 *Cf. n.*   204 unkind: *unnatural*

'What am I that thou shouldst contemn me this?
Or what great danger dwells upon my suit?
What were thy lips the worse for one poor kiss?
Speak, fair; but speak fair words, or else be mute: 208
   Give me one kiss, I'll give it thee again,
   And one for interest, if thou wilt have twain.

'Fie! lifeless picture, cold and senseless stone,
Well-painted idol, image dull and dead,   212
Statue contenting but the eye alone,
Thing like a man, but of no woman bred:
   Thou art no man, though of a man's complexion,
   For men will kiss even by their own direction.'   216

This said, impatience chokes her pleading tongue,
And swelling passion doth provoke a pause;
Red cheeks and fiery eyes blaze forth her wrong;
Being judge in love, she cannot right her cause: 220
   And now she weeps, and now she fain would speak,
   And now her sobs do her intendments break.

Sometimes she shakes her head, and then his hand;
Now gazeth she on him, now on the ground;   224
Sometimes her arms infold him like a band:
She would, he will not in her arms be bound;
   And when from thence he struggles to be gone,
   She locks her lily fingers one in one.   228

'Fondling,' she saith, 'since I have hemm'd thee here
Within the circuit of this ivory pale,
I'll be a park, and thou shalt be my deer;
Feed where thou wilt, on mountain or in dale: 232
   Graze on my lips, and if those hills be dry,
   Stray lower, where the pleasant fountains lie.

205 this: *thus*   219 blaze: *publish*
222 her intendments: *what she means to say*
229 Fondling: *darling*   231 deer; *cf. n.*

'Within this limit is relief enough,
Sweet bottom-grass and high delightful plain,   236
Round rising hillocks, brakes obscure and rough,
To shelter thee from tempest and from rain:
 Then be my deer, since I am such a park;
  No dog shall rouse thee, though a thousand
  bark.'   240

At this Adonis smiles as in disdain,
That in each cheek appears a pretty dimple:
Love made those hollows, if himself were slain,
He might be buried in a tomb so simple;   244
 Foreknowing well, if there he came to lie,
 Why, there Love liv'd and there he could not die.

These lovely caves, these round enchanting pits,
Open'd their mouths to swallow Venus' liking.   248
Being mad before, how doth she now for wits?
Struck dead at first, what needs a second striking?
 Poor queen of love, in thine own law forlorn,
 To love a cheek that smiles at thee in scorn!   252

Now which way shall she turn? what shall she say?
Her words are done, her woes the more increasing;
The time is spent, her object will away,
And from her twining arms doth urge releasing: 256
 'Pity,' she cries; 'some favour, some remorse!'
 Away he springs, and hasteth to his horse.

But, lo! from forth a copse that neighbours by,
A breeding jennet, lusty, young, and proud,   260
Adonis' trampling courser doth espy,
And forth she rushes, snorts and neighs aloud:

235 relief; *cf. n.*   236 bottom-grass: *grass growing in the valleys*
240 rouse; *cf. n.*
257 remorse: *commiseration*   247 caves; *cf. n.*
           259-262 *Cf. n.*

The strong-neck'd steed, being tied unto a tree,
Breaketh his rein, and to her straight goes he.   264

Imperiously he leaps, he neighs, he bounds,
And now his woven girths he breaks asunder;
The bearing earth with his hard hoof he wounds,
Whose hollow womb resounds like heaven's thun-
      der;   268
   The iron bit he crushes 'tween his teeth,
   Controlling what he was controlled with.

His ears up-prick'd; his braided hanging mane
Upon his compass'd crest now stand on end;   272
His nostrils drink the air, and forth again,
As from a furnace, vapours doth he send:
   His eye, which scornfully glisters like fire,
   Shows his hot courage and his high desire.   276

Sometime he trots, as if he told the steps,
With gentle majesty and modest pride;
Anon he rears upright, curvets and leaps,
As who should say, 'Lo! thus my strength is tried; 280
   And this I do to captivate the eye
   Of the fair breeder that is standing by.'

What recketh he his rider's angry stir,
His flattering 'Holla,' or his 'Stand, I say'?   284
What cares he now for curb or pricking spur?
For rich caparisons or trapping gay?
   He sees his love, and nothing else he sees,
   Nor nothing else with his proud sight agrees.   288

263, 264 *Cf. n.*   272 compass'd: *curved*
279 curvets; *cf. n.*   282 breeder: *female*
283 recketh: *cares for*   stir: *agitation*
286 caparisons or trapping; *cf. n.*

Look, when a painter would surpass the life,
In limning out a well-proportion'd steed,
His art with nature's workmanship at strife,
As if the dead the living should exceed;   292
 So did this horse excel a common one,
 In shape, in courage, colour, pace and bone.

Round-hoof'd, short-jointed, fetlocks shag and long,
Broad breast, full eye, small head, and nostril wide, 296
High crest, short ears, straight legs and passing
  strong,
Thin mane, thick tail, broad buttock, tender hide:
 Look, what a horse should have he did not lack,
 Save a proud rider on so proud a back.   300

Sometimes he scuds far off, and there he stares;
Anon he starts at stirring of a feather;
To bid the wind a base he now prepares,
And whe'r he run or fly they know not whether;   304
 For through his mane and tail the high wind sings,
 Fanning the hairs, who wave like feather'd wings.

He looks upon his love, and neighs unto her;
She answers him as if she knew his mind;   308
Being proud, as females are, to see him woo her,
She puts on outward strangeness, seems unkind,
 Spurns at his love and scorns the heat he feels,
 Beating his kind embracements with her heels.   312

Then, like a melancholy malcontent,
He vails his tail that, like a falling plume
Cool shadow to his melting buttock lent:

289-292 *Cf. n.*   295-298 *Cf. n.*
295 shag: *hairy*   297 passing: *exceedingly*
303 To bid . . . base; *cf. n.*
304 whe'r: *whether*   whether: *which of the two*
310 strangeness: *coldness*
314 vails: *lowers*

He stamps, and bites the poor flies in his fume. 316
　His love, perceiving how he was enrag'd,
　Grew kinder, and his fury was assuag'd.

His testy master goeth about to take him;
When lo! the unback'd breeder, full of fear, 320
Jealous of catching, swiftly doth forsake him,
With her the horse, and left Adonis there.
　As they were mad, unto the wood they hie them,
　Out-stripping crows that strive to over-fly them. 324

All swoln with chafing, down Adonis sits,
Banning his boisterous and unruly beast:
And now the happy season once more fits,
That love-sick Love by pleading may be blest; 328
　For lovers say, the heart hath treble wrong
　When it is barr'd the aidance of the tongue.

An oven that is stopp'd, or river stay'd,
Burneth more hotly, swelleth with more rage: 332
So of concealed sorrow may be said;
Free vent of words love's fire doth assuage;
　But when the heart's attorney once is mute,
　The client breaks, as desperate in his suit. 336

He sees her coming, and begins to glow,—
Even as a dying coal revives with wind,—
And with his bonnet hides his angry brow;
Looks on the dull earth with disturbed mind, 340
　Taking no notice that she is so nigh,
　For all askance he holds her in his eye.

O! what a sight it was, wistly to view
How she came stealing to the wayward boy; 344

316 fume: *rage*　　326 Banning: *cursing*　　330 aidance: *help*
329-336 *Cf. n.*
342 *Cf. n.*　　　　　　335 heart's attorney; *cf. n.*
　　　　　　　　　　343 wistly: *attentively*

To note the fighting conflict of her hue,
How white and red each other did destroy:
   But now her cheek was pale, and by and by
   It flash'd forth fire, as lightning from the sky. 348

Now was she just before him as he sat,
And like a lowly lover down she kneels;
With one fair hand she heaveth up his hat,
Her other tender hand his fair cheek feels: 352
   His tenderer cheek receives her soft hand's print,
   As apt as new-fall'n snow takes any dint.

O, what a war of looks was then between them!
Her eyes petitioners to his eyes suing; 356
His eyes saw her eyes as they had not seen them;
Her eyes woo'd still, his eyes disdain'd the wooing:
   And all this dumb play had his acts made plain
   With tears, which, chorus-like, her eyes did rain. 360

Full gently now she takes him by the hand,
A lily prison'd in a gaol of snow,
Or ivory in an alablaster band;
So white a friend engirts so white a foe: 364
   This beauteous combat, wilful and unwilling,
   Show'd like two silver doves that sit a-billing.

Once more the engine of her thoughts began:
'O fairest mover on this mortal round, 368
Would thou wert as I am, and I a man,
My heart all whole as thine, thy heart my wound;
   For one sweet look thy help I would assure thee,
   Though nothing but my body's bane would cure
     thee.' 372

354 dint: *impression*   359, 360 *Cf. n.*
363 alablaster: *alabaster, a stalagmitic white stone*
364 engirts: *encircles*   367 engine; *cf. n.*
368 round: *globe (the earth)*   370 *Cf. n.*   372 bane: *ruin*

'Give me my hand,' saith he, 'why dost thou feel it?'
'Give me my heart,' saith she, 'and thou shalt have it;
O! give it me, lest thy hard heart do steel it,
And being steel'd, soft sighs can never grave it:⠀⠀⠀376
⠀⠀Then love's deep groans I never shall regard,
⠀⠀Because Adonis' heart hath made mine hard.'

'For shame,' he cries, 'let go, and let me go;
My day's delight is past, my horse is gone,⠀⠀⠀380
And 'tis your fault I am bereft him so:
I pray you hence, and leave me here alone:
⠀⠀For all my mind, my thought, my busy care,
⠀⠀Is how to get my palfrey from the mare.'⠀⠀⠀384

Thus she replies: 'Thy palfrey, as he should,
Welcomes the warm approach of sweet desire:
Affection is a coal that must be cool'd;
Else, suffer'd, it will set the heart on fire:⠀⠀⠀388
⠀⠀The sea hath bounds, but deep desire hath none;
⠀⠀Therefore no marvel though thy horse be gone.

'How like a jade he stood, tied to the tree,
Servilely master'd with a leathern rein!⠀⠀⠀392
But when he saw his love, his youth's fair fee,
He held such petty bondage in disdain;
⠀⠀Throwing the base thong from his bending crest,
⠀⠀Enfranchising his mouth, his back, his breast.⠀⠀⠀396

'Who sees his true-love in her naked bed,
Teaching the sheets a whiter hue than white,
But, when his glutton eye so full hath fed,
His other agents aim at like delight?⠀⠀⠀400
⠀⠀Who is so faint, that dare not be so bold
⠀⠀To touch the fire, the weather being cold?

375 steel; *cf. n.*⠀⠀⠀⠀⠀⠀⠀⠀⠀⠀⠀⠀⠀376 grave: *engrave*
388 suffer'd: *allowed to burn*⠀⠀⠀⠀⠀⠀396 Enfranchising: *liberating*
397 naked bed; *cf. n.*

'Let me excuse thy courser, gentle boy;
And learn of him, I heartily beseech thee,   404
To take advantage on presented joy;
Though I were dumb, yet his proceedings teach thee.
  O learn to love; the lesson is but plain,
    And once made perfect, never lost again.'   408

'I know not love,' quoth he, 'nor will not know it,
Unless it be a boar, and then I chase it;
'Tis much to borrow, and I will not owe it;
My love to love is love but to disgrace it;   412
  For I have heard it is a life in death,
    That laughs and weeps, and all but with a breath.

'Who wears a garment shapeless and unfinish'd?
Who plucks the bud before one leaf put forth?   416
If springing things be any jot diminish'd,
They wither in their prime, prove nothing worth:
  The colt that's back'd and burthen'd being young
    Loseth his pride and never waxeth strong.   420

'You hurt my hand with wringing; let us part,
And leave this idle theme, this bootless chat:
Remove your siege from my unyielding heart;
To love's alarms it will not ope the gate: 424
  Dismiss your vows, your feigned tears, your flattery;
    For where a heart is hard, they make no battery.'

'What! canst thou talk?' quoth she, 'hast thou a tongue?
O, would thou hadst not, or I had no hearing!   428
Thy mermaid's voice hath done me double wrong;

I had my load before, now press'd with bearing:
　Melodious discord, heavenly tune, harsh-sounding,
　Ear's deep-sweet music, and heart's deep-sore
　　wounding.   432

'Had I no eyes, but ears, my ears would love
That inward beauty and invisible;
Or were I deaf, thy outward parts would move
Each part in me that were but sensible: 436
　Though neither eyes nor ears, to hear nor see,
　Yet should I be in love by touching thee.

'Say, that the sense of feeling were bereft me,
And that I could not see, nor hear, nor touch,   440
And nothing but the very smell were left me,
Yet would my love to thee be still as much;
　For from the still'tory of thy face excelling
　Comes breath perfum'd that breedeth love by smell-
　　ing.   444

'But O! what banquet wert thou to the taste,
Being nurse and feeder of the other four;
Would they not wish the feast might ever last,
And bid Suspicion double-lock the door,   448
　Lest Jealousy, that sour unwelcome guest,
　Should, by his stealing in, disturb the feast?'

Once more the ruby-colour'd portal open'd,
Which to his speech did honey passage yield;   452
Like a red morn, that ever yet betoken'd
Wrack to the seaman, tempest to the field,
　Sorrow to shepherds, woe unto the birds,
　Gusts and foul flaws to herdmen and to herds.   456

430 press'd: *oppressed, crushed*　　　　　433-450 *Cf. n.*
436 sensible: *capable of sensation*　　443 still'tory: *still (alembic)*
446 four: *four senses*　　　　　　　　　449 Jealousy: *Envy*
456 flaws: *sudden gusts*

This ill presage advisedly she marketh:
Even as the wind is hush'd before it raineth,
Or as the wolf doth grin before he barketh,
Or as the berry breaks before it staineth,　　　460
　　Or like the deadly bullet of a gun,
　　His meaning struck her ere his words begun.

And at his look she flatly falleth down,
For looks kill love and love by looks reviveth;　　464
A smile recures the wounding of a frown;
But blessed bankrupt, that by love so thriveth!
　　The silly boy, believing she is dead,
　　Claps her pale cheek, till clapping makes it red; 468

And all-amaz'd brake off his late intent,
For sharply he did think to reprehend her,
Which cunning love did wittily prevent:
Fair fall the wit that can so well defend her!　　472
　　For on the grass she lies as she were slain,
　　Till his breath breatheth life in her again.

He wrings her nose, he strikes her on the cheeks,
He bends her fingers, holds her pulses hard,　　476
He chafes her lips; a thousand ways he seeks
To mend the hurt that his unkindness marr'd:
　　He kisses her; and she, by her good will,
　　Will never rise, so he will kiss her still.　　480

The night of sorrow now is turn'd to day:
Her two blue windows faintly she up-heaveth,
Like the fair sun, when in his fresh array
He cheers the morn and all the earth relieveth:　　484
　　And as the bright sun glorifies the sky,
　　So is her face illumin'd with her eye;

457 advisedly: *heedfully*　　　　　　465 recures: *cures*
472 *Cf. n.*　　　　　　　　　　　　478 *Cf. n.*
479 by her good will: *of her own accord*　　482 windows; *cf. n.*

Whose beams upon his hairless face are fix'd,
As if from thence they borrow'd all their shine.　488
Were never four such lamps together mix'd,
Had not his clouded with his brows' repine;
　　But hers, which through the crystal tears gave light,
　　Shone like the moon in water seen by night.　492

'O! where am I?' quoth she, 'in earth or heaven,
Or in the ocean drench'd, or in the fire?
What hour is this? or morn or weary even?
Do I delight to die, or life desire?　496
　　But now I liv'd, and life was death's annoy;
　　But now I died, and death was lively joy.

'O! thou didst kill me; kill me once again:
Thy eyes' shrewd tutor, that hard heart of thine,　500
Hath taught them scornful tricks and such disdain
That they have murder'd this poor heart of mine;
　　And these mine eyes, true leaders to their queen,
　　But for thy piteous lips no more had seen.　504

'Long may they kiss each other for this cure!
O, never let their crimson liveries wear!
And as they last, their verdure still endure,
To drive infection from the dangerous year:　508
　　That the star-gazers, having writ on death,
　　May say, the plague is banish'd by thy breath.

'Pure lips, sweet seals in my soft lips imprinted,
What bargains may I make, still to be sealing?　512
To sell myself I can be well contented,
So thou wilt buy and pay and use good dealing;
　　Which purchase if thou make, for fear of slips
　　Set thy seal-manual on my wax-red lips.　516

490 repine: *discontent*　　　　　　494 drench'd: *immersed*
498 lively joy: *life's joy*　506 liveries; *cf. n.*　　wear: *wear out*
507-510 *Cf. n.*　　　　　　　　　507 verdure: *freshness*
515 slips; *cf. n.*　　　　　　　516 wax-red; *cf. n.*

'A thousand kisses buys my heart from me;
And pay them at thy leisure, one by one.
What is ten hundred touches unto thee?
Are they not quickly told and quickly gone?   520
   Say, for non-payment that the debt should double,
   Is twenty hundred kisses such a trouble?'

'Fair queen,' quoth he, 'if any love you owe me,
Measure my strangeness with my unripe years: 524
Before I know myself, seek not to know me;
No fisher but the ungrown fry forbears:
   The mellow plum doth fall, the green sticks fast,
   Or being early pluck'd is sour to taste.   528

'Look! the world's comforter, with weary gait,
His day's hot task hath ended in the west;
The owl, night's herald, shrieks, 'tis very late;
The sheep are gone to fold, birds to their nest,   532
   And coal-black clouds that shadow heaven's light
   Do summon us to part and bid good night.

'Now let me say good night, and so say you;
If you will say so, you shall have a kiss.'   536
'Good night,' quoth she; and ere he says adieu,
The honey fee of parting tender'd is:
   Her arms do lend his neck a sweet embrace;
   Incorporate then they seem, face grows to face.   540

Till, breathless, he disjoin'd, and backward drew
The heavenly moisture, that sweet coral mouth,
Whose precious taste her thirsty lips well knew,
Whereon they surfeit, yet complain on drouth: 544
   He with her plenty press'd, she faint with dearth,
   Their lips together glu'd, fall to the earth.

529 comforter; *cf. n.*

Now quick desire hath caught the yielding prey,
And glutton-like she feeds, yet never filleth;   548
Her lips are conquerors, his lips obey,
Paying what ransom the insulter willeth;
   Whose vulture thought doth pitch the price so high,
    That she will draw his lips' rich treasure dry.   552

And having felt the sweetness of the spoil,
With blindfold fury she begins to forage;
Her face doth reek and smoke, her blood doth boil,
And careless lust stirs up a desperate courage;   556
   Planting oblivion, beating reason back,
    Forgetting shame's pure blush and honour's wrack.

Hot, faint, and weary, with her hard embracing,
Like a wild bird being tam'd with too much han-
    dling,   560
Or as the fleet-foot roe that's tir'd with chasing,
Or like the froward infant still'd with dandling,
   He now obeys, and now no more resisteth,
    While she takes all she can, not all she listeth. 564

What wax so frozen but dissolves with tempering,
And yields at last to every light impression?
Things out of hope are compass'd oft with venturing,
Chiefly in love, whose leave exceeds commission: 568
   Affection faints not like a pale-fac'd coward,
    But then woos best when most his choice is froward.

When he did frown, O! had she then gave over,
Such nectar from his lips she had not suck'd.   572
Foul words and frowns must not repel a lover;

558 wrack: *ruin*   565, 566 *Cf. n.*
570 choice: *the person chosen*   571 gave: *given*

What though the rose have prickles, yet 'tis pluck'd:
  Were beauty under twenty locks kept fast,
    Yet love breaks through and picks them all at
      last.   576

For pity now she can no more detain him;
The poor fool prays her that he may depart:
She is resolv'd no longer to restrain him,
Bids him farewell, and look well to her heart,   580
  The which, by Cupid's bow she doth protest,
    He carries thence incaged in his breast.

'Sweet boy,' she says, 'this night I'll waste in sorrow,
For my sick heart commands mine eyes to watch. 584
Tell me, Love's master, shall we meet to-morrow?
Say, shall we? shall we? wilt thou make the match?'
  He tells her, no; to-morrow he intends
    To hunt the boar with certain of his friends.   588

'The boar!' quoth she; whereat a sudden pale,
Like lawn being spread upon the blushing rose,
Usurps her cheek, she trembles at his tale,
And on his neck her yoking arms she throws: 592
  She sinketh down, still hanging by his neck,
    He on her belly falls, she on her back.

Now is she in the very lists of love,
Her champion mounted for the hot encounter: 596
All is imaginary she doth prove,
He will not manage her, although he mount her;
  That worse than Tantalus' is her annoy,
    To clip Elysium and to lack her joy.   600

586 make the match: *ratify the bargain*   589, 590 *Cf. n.*
589 pale: *paleness*   598 manage; *cf. n.*
600 clip: *embrace*

He cranks and crosses with a thousand doubles:
　The many musits through the which he goes
　Are like a labyrinth to amaze his foes. 684

Sometime he runs among a flock of sheep,
To make the cunning hounds mistake their smell,
And sometime where earth-delving conies keep,
To stop the loud pursuers in their yell, 688
　And sometime sorteth with a herd of deer;
　Danger deviseth shifts; wit waits on fear:

For there his smell with others being mingled,
The hot scent-snuffing hounds are driven to doubt, 692
Ceasing their clamorous cry till they have singled
With much ado the cold fault cleanly out;
　Then do they spend their mouths: Echo replies,
　As if another chase were in the skies. 696

By this, poor Wat, far off upon a hill,
Stands on his hinder legs with listening ear,
To hearken if his foes pursue him still:
Anon their loud alarums he doth hear; 700
　And now his grief may be compared well
　To one sore sick that hears the passing-bell.

Then shalt thou see the dew-bedabbled wretch
Turn, and return, indenting with the way; 704
Each envious briar his weary legs doth scratch,
Each shadow makes him stop, each murmur stay:
　For misery is trodden on by many,
　And being low never reliev'd by any. 708

Even so poor birds, deceiv'd with painted grapes,
Do surfeit by the eye and pine the maw,
Even so she languisheth in her mishaps,
As those poor birds that helpless berries saw. 604
　The warm effects which she in him finds missing,
　She seeks to kindle with continual kissing.

But all in vain; good queen, it will not be;
She hath assay'd as much as may be prov'd; 608
Her pleading hath deserv'd a greater fee;
She's Love, she loves, and yet she is not lov'd.
　'Fie, fie!' he says, 'you crush me; let me go;
　You have no reason to withhold me so.' 612

'Thou hadst been gone,' quoth she, 'sweet boy, ere this,
But that thou told'st me thou wouldst hunt the boar.
O, be advis'd! thou know'st not what it is
With javelin's point a churlish swine to gore, 616
　Whose tushes never sheath'd he whetteth still,
　Like to a mortal butcher, bent to kill.

'On his bow-back he hath a battle set
Of bristly pikes, that ever threat his foes; 620
His eyes like glow-worms shine when he doth fret;
His snout digs sepulchres where'er he goes;
　Being mov'd, he strikes whate'er is in his way,
　And whom he strikes his crooked tushes slay. 624

'His brawny sides, with hairy bristles arm'd,
Are better proof than thy spear's point can enter;
His short thick neck cannot be easily harm'd;

---

cranks: *runs in and out*　　doubles: *sudden turns*
　musits; *cf. n.*　　　　　　　　　685-688 *Cf. n.*
, 694 till . . . out; *cf. n.*　　695 spend their mouths; *cf. n.*
　Cf. n.　　　　　　　　　　　697-699 *Cf. n.*
, 702 *Cf. n.*　　　　　　　　　704 indenting; *cf. n.*

601 painted grapes; *cf. n.*　　　　　　　602 pine: *starve*
604 helpless: *which could not afford any help*
608 assay'd . . . prov'd; *cf. n.*
615 advis'd: *prudent*　　　　　　　　　　615-618 *Cf. n.*
618 mortal: *death-giving*　　　　　　　617 tushes: *tusks*
619 battle: *army*　　　623 mov'd: *angry*　　619-630 *Cf. n.*
　　　　　　　　　　　　　　　　　　　　626 *Cf. n.*

Being ireful, on the lion he will venture: 628
    The thorny brambles and embracing bushes,
    As fearful of him part, through whom he rushes.

'Alas! he naught esteems that face of thine,
To which Love's eyes pay tributary gazes;   632
Nor thy soft hands, sweet lips, and crystal eyne,
Whose full perfection all the world amazes;
    But having thee at vantage, wondrous dread!
    Would root these beauties as he roots the mead. 636

'O, let him keep his loathsome cabin still!
Beauty hath naught to do with such foul fiends:
Come not within his danger by thy will;
They that thrive well take counsel of their friends. 640
    When thou didst name the boar, not to dissemble,
    I fear'd thy fortune, and my joints did tremble.

'Didst thou not mark my face? was it not white?
Saw'st thou not signs of fear lurk in mine eye?   644
Grew I not faint? And fell I not downright?
Within my bosom, whereon thou dost lie,
    My boding heart pants, beats, and takes no rest,
    But, like an earthquake, shakes thee on my
    breast.   648

'For where Love reigns, disturbing Jealousy
Doth call himself Affection's sentinel;
Gives false alarms, suggesteth mutiny,
And in a peaceful hour doth cry "Kill, kill!"   652
    Distempering gentle Love in his desire,
    As air and water do abate the fire.

'This sour informer, this bate-breeding
This canker that eats up Love's tender
This carry-tale, dissentious Jealousy,
That sometime true news, sometime fal
    Knocks at my heart, and whispers in
    That if I love thee, I thy death shoul

'And more than so, presenteth to mine
The picture of an angry-chafing boar,
Under whose sharp fangs on his back do
An image like thyself, all stain'd with
    Whose blood upon the fresh flowers
    Doth make them droop with grief
    head.

'What should I do, seeing thee so indeed
That tremble at the imagination?
The thought of it doth make my faint
And fear doth teach it divination:
    I prophesy thy death, my living sorro
    If thou encounter with the boar to-m

'But if thou needs wilt hunt, be rul'd by
Uncouple at the timorous flying hare,
Or at the fox which lives by subtilty,
Or at the roe which no encounter dare:
    Pursue these fearful creatures o'er th
    And on thy well-breath'd horse k
    hounds.

'And when thou hast on foot the purbli
Mark the poor wretch, to overshoot his
How he outruns the winds, and with wh

---

631 *Cf. n.*
639 within his danger: *within his dangerous reach*   636 root: *uproot*
652 Kill, kill; *cf. n.*   653 Distempering: *allaying*

655 bate: *strife*   656
673-678 *Cf. n.*   673-708 *Cf. n.*   674 Uncoupl
680 overshoot: *pass swiftly over*

'Lie quietly, and hear a little more;
Nay, do not struggle, for thou shalt not rise:
To make thee hate the hunting of the boar,
Unlike myself thou hear'st me moralize,   712
    Applying this to that, and so to so;
    For love can comment upon every woe.

'Where did I leave?' 'No matter where,' quoth he;
'Leave me, and then the story aptly ends: 716
The night is spent,' 'Why, what of that?' quoth she.
'I am,' quoth he, 'expected of my friends;
    And now 'tis dark, and going I shall fall.'
    'In night,' quoth she, 'desire sees best of all.'   720

'But if thou fall, O! then imagine this,
The earth, in love with thee, thy footing trips,
And all is but to rob thee of a kiss.
Rich preys make true men thieves; so do thy lips   724
    Make modest Dian cloudy and forlorn,
    Lest she should steal a kiss and die forsworn.

'Now of this dark night I perceive the reason:
Cynthia for shame obscures her silver shine,   728
Till forging Nature be condemn'd of treason,
For stealing moulds from heaven that were divine;
    Wherein she fram'd thee in high heaven's despite,
    To shame the sun by day and her by night.   732

'And therefore hath she brib'd the Destinies,
To cross the curious workmanship of nature,
To mingle beauty with infirmities,
And pure perfection with impure defeature;   736
    Making it subject to the tyranny
    Of mad mischances and much misery;

720 *Cf. n.*   724 true: *honest*   725 cloudy; *cf. n.*
726 forsworn; *cf. n.*   730 moulds; *cf. n.*
734 cross: *injure*   736 defeature: *defacement*

'As burning fevers, agues pale and faint,
Life-poisoning pestilence and frenzies wood,   740
The marrow-eating sickness, whose attaint
Disorder breeds by heating of the blood;
   Surfeits, imposthumes, grief, and damn'd despair,
   Swear nature's death for framing thee so fair.   744

'And not the least of all these maladies
But in one minute's fight brings beauty under:
Both favour, savour, hue, and qualities,
Whereat the impartial gazer late did wonder,   748
   Are on the sudden wasted, thaw'd and done,
   As mountain-snow melts with the mid-day sun.

'Therefore, despite of fruitless chastity,
Love-lacking vestals and self-loving nuns,   752
That on the earth would breed a scarcity
And barren dearth of daughters and of sons,
   Be prodigal: the lamp that burns by night
   Dries up his oil to lend the world his light.   756

'What is thy body but a swallowing grave,
Seeming to bury that posterity
Which by the rights of time thou needs must have,
If thou destroy them not in dark obscurity?   760
   If so, the world will hold thee in disdain,
   Sith in thy pride so fair a hope is slain.

'So in thyself thyself art made away;
A mischief worse than civil home-bred strife,   764
Or theirs whose desperate hands themselves do slay,
Or butcher-sire that reaves his son of life.
   Foul-cankering rust the hidden treasure frets,
   But gold that's put to use more gold begets.'   768

740 wood: *mad*   741 attaint: *infection*
743 imposthumes: *abscesses*   747 favour: *appearance*
751 fruitless; *cf. n.*   757, 758 *Cf. n.*
766 reaves: *bereaves*   768 *Cf. n.*

'Nay then,' quoth Adon, 'you will fall again
Into your idle over-handled theme;
The kiss I gave you is bestow'd in vain,
And all in vain you strive against the stream;   772
    For by this black-fac'd night, desire's foul nurse,
    Your treatise makes me like you worse and worse.

'If love have lent you twenty thousand tongues,
And every tongue more moving than your own,   776
Bewitching like the wanton mermaid's songs,
Yet from mine ear the tempting tune is blown;
    For know, my heart stands armed in mine ear,
    And will not let a false sound enter there;   780

'Lest the deceiving harmony should run
Into the quiet closure of my breast;
And then my little heart were quite undone,
In his bedchamber to be barr'd of rest.   784
    No, lady, no; my heart longs not to groan,
    But soundly sleeps, while now it sleeps alone.

'What have you urg'd that I cannot reprove?
The path is smooth that leadeth on to danger;   788
I hate not love, but your device in love,
That lends embracements unto every stranger.
    You do it for increase: O strange excuse!
    When reason is the bawd to lust's abuse.   792

'Call it not love, for Love to heaven is fled,
Since sweating Lust on earth usurp'd his name;
Under whose simple semblance he hath fed
Upon fresh beauty, blotting it with blame;   796
    Which the hot tyrant stains and soon bereaves,
    As caterpillars do the tender leaves.

774 treatise: *discourse*   782 closure: *enclosure*
784 barr'd: *shut out from, deprived*   787 reprove: *disprove*

'Love comforteth like sunshine after rain,
But Lust's effect is tempest after sun;   800
Love's gentle spring doth always fresh remain,
Lust's winter comes ere summer half be done.
    Love surfeits not, Lust like a glutton dies;
    Love is all truth, Lust full of forged lies.   804

'More I could tell, but more I dare not say;
The text is old, the orator too green.
Therefore, in sadness, now I will away;
My face is full of shame, my heart of teen: 808
    Mine ears, that to your wanton talk attended,
    Do burn themselves for having so offended.'

With this he breaketh from the sweet embrace
Of those fair arms which bound him to her breast, 812
And homeward through the dark laund runs apace;
Leaves Love upon her back deeply distress'd.
    Look, how a bright star shooteth from the sky,
    So glides he in the night from Venus' eye;   816

Which after him she darts, as one on shore
Gazing upon a late-embarked friend,
Till the wild waves will have him seen no more,
Whose ridges with the meeting clouds contend: 820
    So did the merciless and pitchy night
    Fold in the object that did feed her sight.

Whereat amaz'd, as one that unaware
Hath dropp'd a precious jewel in the flood,   824
Or stonish'd as night-wanderers often are,
Their light blown out in some mistrustful wood;
    Even so confounded in the dark she lay,
    Having lost the fair discovery of her way.   828

808 teen: *grief*   813 laund: *glade*   825 stonish'd: *bewildered*
826 mistrustful: *causing mistrust*   828 discovery; *cf. n.*

And now she beats her heart, whereat it groans,
That all the neighbour caves, as seeming troubled,
Make verbal repetition of her moans;
Passion on passion deeply is redoubled: 832
   'Ay me!' she cries, and twenty times, 'Woe, woe!'
   And twenty echoes twenty times cry so.

She marking them, begins a wailing note,
And sings extemporally a woeful ditty;   836
How love makes young men thrall and old men dote;
How love is wise in folly, foolish-witty:
   Her heavy anthem still concludes in woe,
   And still the choir of echoes answer so.   840

Her song was tedious, and outwore the night,
For lovers' hours are long, though seeming short:
If pleas'd themselves, others, they think, delight
In such like circumstance, with such like sport: 844
   Their copious stories, oftentimes begun,
   End without audience, and are never done.

For who hath she to spend the night withal,
But idle sounds resembling parasites;   848
Like shrill-tongu'd tapsters answering every call,
Soothing the humour of fantastic wits?
   She says, ''Tis so': they answer all, ''Tis so';
   And would say after her, if she said 'No.'   852

Lo! here the gentle lark, weary of rest,
From his moist cabinet mounts up on high,
And wakes the morning, from whose silver breast
The sun ariseth in his majesty;   856
   Who doth the world so gloriously behold,
   That cedar-tops and hills seem burnish'd gold

832 Passion: *lament*   837 thrall: *bs slaves*
844 circumstance: *circuitous discourse* 848 parasites; *cf. n.*
854 cabinet; *cf. n.*

Venus salutes him with this fair good morrow:
'O thou clear god, and patron of all light,   860
From whom each lamp and shining star doth borrow
The beauteous influence that makes him bright,
 There lives a son that suck'd an earthly mother,
 May lend thee light, as thou dost lend to other.'   864

This said, she hasteth to a myrtle grove,
Musing the morning is so much o'erworn,
And yet she hears no tidings of her love;
She hearkens for his hounds and for his horn: 868
 Anon she hears them chant it lustily,
 And all in haste she coasteth to the cry.

And as she runs, the bushes in the way
Some catch her by the neck, some kiss her face,   872
Some twine about her thigh to make her stay:
She wildly breaketh from their strict embrace,
 Like a milch doe, whose swelling dugs do ache,
 Hasting to feed her fawn hid in some brake.   876

By this she hears the hounds are at a bay;
Whereat she starts, like one that spies an adder
Wreath'd up in fatal folds just in his way,
The fear whereof doth make him shake and shud-
  der;   880
 Even so the timorous yelping of the hounds
 Appals her senses, and her spirit confounds.

For now she knows it is no gentle chase,
But the blunt boar, rough bear, or lion proud,   884
Because the cry remaineth in one place,

864 other: *others*   866 Musing: *wondering*
870 coasteth: *approaches*   877 at a bay; *cf. n.*
883, 884 *Cf. n.*

Where fearfully the dogs exclaim aloud:
   Finding their enemy to be so curst,
   They all strain courtesy who shall cope him first. 888

This dismal cry rings sadly in her ear,
Through which it enters to surprise her heart;
Who, overcome by doubt and bloodless fear,
With cold-pale weakness numbs each feeling part; 892
   Like soldiers, when their captain once doth yield,
   They basely fly and dare not stay the field.

Thus stands she in a trembling ecstasy,
Till, cheering up her senses all dismay'd,   896
She tells them 'tis a causeless fantasy,
And childish error, that they are afraid;
   Bids them leave quaking, bids them fear no more:
   And with that word she spied the hunted boar,   900

Whose frothy mouth bepainted all with red,
Like milk and blood being mingled both together,
A second fear through all her sinews spread,
Which madly hurries her she knows not whither: 904
   This way she runs, and now she will no further,
   But back retires to rate the boar for murther.

A thousand spleens bear her a thousand ways,
She treads the path that she untreads again;   908
Her more than haste is mated with delays,
Like the proceedings of a drunken brain,
   Full of respects, yet nought at all respecting,
   In hand with all things, nought at all effecting. 912

887 curst: *peevish*
888 strain courtesy; *cf. n.*   cope: *encounter*
889 cry; *cf. n.*
895 ecstasy: *excitement*   891, 892 *Cf. n.*
909 mated: *baffled*   907 spleens: *whims, sudden motions*
912 In hand with: *undertaking*   911 respects: *considerations*

Here kennel'd in a brake she finds a hound,
And asks the weary caitiff for his master,
And there another licking of his wound,
'Gainst venom'd sores the only sovereign plaster;   916
   And here she meets another sadly scowling,
    To whom she speaks, and he replies with howling.

When he hath ceas'd his ill-resounding noise,
Another flap-mouth'd mourner, black and grim,   920
Against the welkin volleys out his voice;
Another and another answer him,
   Clapping their proud tails to the ground below,
    Shaking their scratch'd ears, bleeding as they go. 924

Look, how the world's poor people are amaz'd
At apparitions, signs, and prodigies,
Whereon with fearful eyes they long have gaz'd,
Infusing them with dreadful prophecies;   928
   So she at these sad sighs draws up her breath,
    And, sighing it again, exclaims on Death.

'Hard-favour'd tyrant, ugly, meagre, lean,
Hateful divorce of love,'—thus chides she Death,— 932
'Grim-grinning ghost, earth's worm, what dost thou
    mean
To stifle beauty and to steal his breath,
   Who when he liv'd, his breath and beauty set
   Gloss on the rose, smell to the violet?   936

'If he be dead, O no! it cannot be,
Seeing his beauty, thou shouldst strike at it;
O yes! it may; thou hast no eyes to see,
But hatefully at random dost thou hit.   940
   Thy mark is feeble age, but thy false dart
   Mistakes that aim and cleaves an infant's heart.

920 flap-mouth'd; *cf. n.*   933 worm; *cf. n.*

'Hadst thou but bid beware, then he had spoke,
And, hearing him, thy power had lost his power. 944
The Destinies will curse thee for this stroke;
They bid thee crop a weed, thou pluck'st a flower.
  Love's golden arrow at him should have fled,
  And not Death's ebon dart, to strike him dead. 948

'Dost thou drink tears, that thou provok'st such weep-
    ing?
What may a heavy groan advantage thee?
Why hast thou cast into eternal sleeping
Those eyes that taught all other eyes to see? 952
  Now Nature cares not for thy mortal vigour,
  Since her best work is ruin'd with thy rigour.'

Here overcome, as one full of despair,
She vail'd her eyelids, who, like sluices, stopp'd 956
The crystal tide that from her two cheeks fair
In the sweet channel of her bosom dropp'd;
  But through the flood-gates breaks the silver rain,
  And with his strong course opens them again. 960

O, how her eyes and tears did lend and borrow!
Her eye seen in the tears, tears in her eye;
Both crystals, where they view'd each other's sorrow,
Sorrow that friendly sighs sought still to dry; 964
  But like a stormy day, now wind, now rain,
  Sighs dry her cheeks, tears make them wet again.

Variable passions throng her constant woe,
As striving who should best become her grief; 968
All entertain'd, each passion labours so,
That every present sorrow seemeth chief,
  But none is best; then join they all together,
  Like many clouds consulting for foul weather. 972

944 his: *its*   947 golden arrow; *cf. n.*
948 ebon: *ebony (i.e. black)*   956 vail'd: *let fall*

By this, far off she hears some huntsman holla;
A nurse's song ne'er pleas'd her babe so well:
The dire imagination she did follow
This sound of hope doth labour to expel;   976
    For now reviving joy bids her rejoice,
    And flatters her it is Adonis' voice.

Whereat her tears began to turn their tide,
Being prison'd in her eye, like pearls in glass;   980
Yet sometimes falls an orient drop beside,
Which her cheek melts, as scorning it should pass,
    To wash the foul face of the sluttish ground,
    Who is but drunken when she seemeth drown'd. 984

O hard-believing love! how strange it seems
Not to believe, and yet too credulous;
Thy weal and woe are both of them extremes;
Despair and hope make thee ridiculous: 988
    The one doth flatter thee in thoughts unlikely,
    In likely thoughts the other kills thee quickly.

Now she unweaves the web that she hath wrought:
Adonis lives, and Death is not to blame;   992
It was not she that call'd him all to naught,
Now she adds honours to his hateful name;
    She clepes him king of graves, and grave for kings,
    Imperious supreme of all mortal things.   996

'No, no,' quoth she, 'sweet Death, I did but jest;
Yet pardon me, I felt a kind of fear
Whenas I met the boar, that bloody beast,
Which knows no pity, but is still severe;   1000
    Then, gentle shadow,—truth I must confess,—
    I rail'd on thee, fearing my love's decease.

981 orient drop: *pearl*   993 *Cf. n.*
995 clepes: *calls*   996 Imperious supreme: *imperial chief*

"'Tis not my fault: the boar provok'd my tongue;
Be wreak'd on him, invisible commander;   1004
'Tis he, foul creature, that hath done thee wrong;
I did but act, he's author of my slander:
　　Grief hath two tongues: and never woman yet,
　　Could rule them both without ten women's wit.' 1008

Thus hoping that Adonis is alive,
Her rash suspect she doth extenuate;
And that his beauty may the better thrive,
With Death she humbly doth insinuate;   1012
　　Tells him of trophies, statues, tombs; and stories
　　His victories, his triumphs, and his glories.

'O Jove!' quoth she, 'how much a fool was I,
To be of such a weak and silly mind   1016
To wail his death who lives and must not die
Till mutual overthrow of mortal kind;
　　For he being dead, with him is beauty slain,
　　And, beauty dead, black chaos comes again.   1020

'Fie, fie, fond love! thou art so full of fear
As one with treasure laden, hemm'd with thieves;
Trifles, unwitnessed with eye or ear,
Thy coward heart with false bethinking grieves.'   1024
　　Even at this word she hears a merry horn,
　　Whereat she leaps that was but late forlorn.

As falcon to the lure, away she flies;
The grass stoops not, she treads on it so light;   1028
And in her haste unfortunately spies

1004 wreak'd: *avenged*　　　　　　1010 suspect: *suspicion*
1012 insinuate: *flatter*　　　　　　1013 trophies; *cf. n.*
1018 mutual: *general*　　　　　　　1027 lure; *cf. n.*
1028 *Cf. r*

The foul boar's conquest on her fair delight;
  Which seen, her eyes, as murder'd with the view,
  Like stars asham'd of day, themselves with-
      drew: 1032

Or, as the snail, whose tender horns being hit,
Shrinks backwards in his shelly cave with pain,
And there, all smother'd up, in shade doth sit,
Long after fearing to creep forth again;   1036
  So, at his bloody view, her eyes are fled
  Into the deep dark cabins of her head:

Where they resign their office and their light
To the disposing of her troubled brain;   1040
Who bids them still consort with ugly night,
And never wound the heart with looks again;
  Who, like a king perplexed in his throne,
  By their suggestion gives a deadly groan,   1044

Whereat each tributary subject quakes;
As when the wind, imprison'd in the ground,
Struggling for passage, earth's foundation shakes,
Which with cold terror doth men's minds confound. 1048
  This mutiny each part doth so surprise
  That from their dark beds once more leap her eyes;

And, being open'd, threw unwilling light
Upon the wide wound that the boar had trench'd   1052
In his soft flank; whose wonted lily white
With purple tears, that his wound wept, was drench'd:
  No flower was nigh, no grass, herb, leaf, or weed,
  But stole his blood and seem'd with him to
      bleed.   1056

1041 consort: *associate*   1052 trench'd: *dug*

This solemn sympathy poor Venus noteth,
Over one shoulder doth she hang her head,
Dumbly she passions, franticly she doteth;
She thinks he could not die, he is not dead: 1060
   Her voice is stopp'd, her joints forget to bow,
   Her eyes are mad that they have wept till now.

Upon his hurt she looks so steadfastly,
That her sight dazzling makes the wound seem
     three; 1064
And then she reprehends her mangling eye,
That makes more gashes where no breach should be:
   His face seems twain, each several limb is doubled;
   For oft the eye mistakes, the brain being trou-
     bled. 1068

'My tongue cannot express my grief for one,
And yet,' quoth she, 'behold two Adons dead!
My sighs are blown away, my salt tears gone,
Mine eyes are turn'd to fire, my heart to lead: 1072
   Heavy heart's lead, melt at mine eyes' red fire!
   So shall I die by drops of hot desire.

'Alas! poor world, what treasure hast thou lost?
What face remains alive that's worth the viewing? 1076
Whose tongue is music now? what canst thou boast
Of things long since, or anything ensuing?
   The flowers are sweet, their colours fresh and trim;
   But true-sweet beauty liv'd and died with him. 1080

'Bonnet nor veil henceforth no creature wear!
Nor sun nor wind will ever strive to kiss you:
Having no fair to lose, you need not fear;

1064 *Cf. n.*   1078 ensuing: *future*
1083 fair: *beauty*

The sun doth scorn you, and the wind doth hiss
    you: 1084
  But when Adonis liv'd, sun and sharp air
  Lurk'd like two thieves, to rob him of his fair:

'And therefore would he put his bonnet on,
Under whose brim the gaudy sun would peep; 1088
The wind would blow it off, and, being gone,
Play with his locks: then would Adonis weep;
  And straight, in pity of his tender years,
    They both would strive who first should dry his
    tears. 1092

'To see his face the lion walk'd along
Behind some hedge, because he would not fear him;
To recreate himself when he hath sung,
The tiger would be tame and gently hear him; 1096
  If he had spoke, the wolf would leave his prey,
  And never fright the silly lamb that day.

'When he beheld his shadow in the brook,
The fishes spread on it their golden gills; 1100
When he was by, the birds such pleasure took,
That some would sing, some other in their bills
  Would bring him mulberries and ripe-red cherries;
  He fed them with his sight, they him with ber-
  ries. 1104

'But this foul, grim, and urchin-snouted boar,
Whose downward eye still looketh for a grave,
Ne'er saw the beauteous livery that he wore;
Witness the entertainment that he gave: 1108
  If he did see his face, why then I know
  He thought to kiss him, and hath kill'd him so.

1094 fear: *scare*   1098 silly: *harmless*   1105 urchin: *hedgehog*
1107 beauteous livery: *outward beauty*   1110 *Cf. n.*

"Tis true, 'tis true; thus was Adonis slain:
He ran upon the boar with his sharp spear,   1112
Who did not whet his teeth at him again,
But by a kiss thought to persuade him there;
   And nuzzling in his flank, the loving swine
   Sheath'd unaware the tusk in his soft groin.   1116

'Had I been tooth'd like him, I must confess,
With kissing him I should have kill'd him first;
But he is dead, and never did he bless
My youth with his; the more am I accurst.'   1120
   With this she falleth in the place she stood,
   And stains her face with his congealed blood.

She looks upon his lips, and they are pale;
She takes him by the hand, and that is cold;   1124
She whispers in his ears a heavy tale,
As if they heard the woeful words she told;
   She lifts the coffer-lids that close his eyes,
   Where, lo! two lamps, burnt out, in darkness
     lies;   1128

Two glasses where herself herself beheld
A thousand times, and now no more reflect;
Their virtue lost, wherein they late excell'd,
And every beauty robb'd of his effect: 1132
   'Wonder of time,' quoth she, 'this is my spite,
   That, thou being dead, the day should yet be light.

'Since thou art dead, lo! here I prophesy,
Sorrow on love hereafter shall attend: 1136
It shall be waited on with jealousy,
Find sweet beginning, but unsavoury end;
   Ne'er settled equally, but high or low;
   That all love's pleasure shall not match his woe. 1140

1115, 1116 *Cf. n.*   1125 heavy: *sad*
1127 coffer-lids; *cf. n.*   1139 settled equally: *evenly balanced*

'It shall be fickle, false, and full of fraud,
Bud and be blasted in a breathing-while;
The bottom poison, and the top o'erstraw'd
With sweets that shall the truest sight beguile: 1144
   The strongest body shall it make most weak,
   Strike the wise dumb and teach the fool to speak.

'It shall be sparing and too full of riot,
Teaching decrepit age to tread the measures;   1148
The staring ruffian shall it keep in quiet,
Pluck down the rich, enrich the poor with treasures;
   It shall be raging mad, and silly mild,
   Make the young old, the old become a child.   1152

'It shall suspect where is no cause of fear;
It shall not fear where it should most mistrust;
It shall be merciful, and too severe,
And most deceiving when it seems most just;   1156
   Perverse it shall be, where it shows most toward,
   Put fear to valour, courage to the coward.

'It shall be cause of war and dire events,
And set dissension 'twixt the son and sire;   1160
Subject and servile to all discontents,
As dry combustious matter is to fire:
   Sith in his prime Death doth my love destroy,
   They that love best their love shall not enjoy.'   1164

By this, the boy that by her side lay kill'd
Was melted like a vapour from her sight,
And in his blood that on the ground lay spill'd,
A purple flower sprung up, chequer'd with white;   1168
   Resembling well his pale cheeks, and the blood
   Which in round drops upon their whiteness stood.

1143 o'erstraw'd: *overstrewn*   1148 measures; *cf. n.*
1157 toward: *yielding*   1162 combustious: *combustible*
1168 purple flower; *cf. n.*

She bows her head, the new-sprung flower to smell,
Comparing it to her Adonis' breath;　　　　　1172
And says within her bosom it shall dwell,
Since he himself is reft from her by death:
　　She crops the stalk, and in the breach appears
　　Green dropping sap, which she compares to
　　　tears.　　　　　　　　　　　　　　　　1176

'Poor flower,' quoth she, 'this was thy father's guise,
Sweet issue of a more sweet-smelling sire
For every little grief to wet his eyes:
To grow unto himself was his desire,　　　　1180
　　And so 'tis thine; but know, it is as good
　　To wither in my breast as in his blood.

'Here was thy father's bed, here in my breast;
Thou art the next of blood, and 'tis thy right:　1184
Lo! in this hollow cradle take thy rest,
My throbbing heart shall rock thee day and night:
　　There shall not be one minute in an hour
　　Wherein I will not kiss my sweet love's flower.'　1188

Thus weary of the world, away she hies,
And yokes her silver doves; by whose swift aid
Their mistress, mounted, through the empty skies
In her light chariot quickly is convey'd;　　　1192
　　Holding their course to Paphos, where their queen
　　Means to immure herself and not be seen.

1193 Paphos; *cf. n.*

FINIS.

The Rape of Lucrece

TO THE RIGHT HONOURABLE HENRY
WRIOTHESLEY

EARL OF SOUTHAMPTON AND BARON OF TICHFIELD.

THE love I dedicate to your lordship is without end; whereof this pamphlet, without beginning, is but a superfluous moiety. The warrant I have of your honourable disposition, not the worth of my untutored 4 lines, makes it assured of acceptance. What I have done is yours; what I have to do is yours; being part in all I have, devoted yours. Were my worth greater, my duty would show greater; meantime, as it is, it 8 is bound to your lordship, to whom I wish long life, still lengthened with happiness.

Your lordship's in all duty,

WILLIAM SHAKESPEARE.

THE ARGUMENT.

LUCIUS TARQUINIUS (for his excessive pride surnamed Superbus), after he had caused his own father-in-law, Servius Tullius, to be cruelly murdered, and contrary to the Roman laws and customs, not requiring or staying for the people's suffrages, had 4 possessed himself of the kingdom, went, accompanied with his sons and other noblemen of Rome, to besiege Ardea. During which siege the principal men 8 of the army meeting one evening at the tent of Sextus Tarquinius, the king's son, in their discourses

1-8 *Cf. n.*   1 Lucius Tarquinius; *cf. n.*   8 Ardea; *cf. n.*

after supper, every one commended the virtues of his
own wife: among whom Collatinus extolled the in- 12
comparable chastity of his wife Lucretia. In that
pleasant humour they all posted to Rome; and in-
tending, by their secret and sudden arrival, to make
trial of that which every one had before avouched, 16
only Collatinus finds his wife—though it were late
in the night—spinning amongst her maids: the other
ladies were all found dancing and revelling, or in
several disports. Whereupon the noblemen yielded 20
Collatinus the victory, and his wife the fame. At
that time Sextus Tarquinius, being inflamed with
Lucrece' beauty, yet smothering his passions for
the present, departed with the rest back to the 24
camp; from whence he shortly after privily with-
drew himself, and was, according to his estate,
royally entertained and lodged by Lucrece at Colla-
tium. The same night he treacherously stealeth into 28
her chamber, violently ravished her, and early in the
morning speedeth away. Lucrece, in this lament-
able plight, hastily dispatcheth messengers, one to
Rome for her father, and another to the camp for 32
Collatine. They came, the one accompanied with
Junius Brutus, the other with Publius Valerius; and
finding Lucrece attired in mourning habit, demanded
the cause of her sorrow. She, first taking an oath of 3ı
them for her revenge, revealed the actor, and the
whole manner of his dealing, and withal suddenly
stabbed herself. Which done, with one consent they
all vowed to root out the whole hated family of the 40
Tarquins; and, bearing the dead body to Rome,
Brutus acquainted the people with the doer and
manner of the vile deed, with a bitter invective

against the tyranny of the king; wherewith the 44 people were so moved, that with one consent and a general acclamation the Tarquins were all exiled, and the state government changed from kings to consuls. 48

The Rape of Lucrece

FROM the besieged Ardea all in post,
Borne by the trustless wings of false desire,
Lust-breathed Tarquin leaves the Roman host,
And to Collatium bears the lightless fire   **4**
Which, in pale embers hid, lurks to aspire,
    And girdle with embracing flames the waist
    Of Collatine's fair love, Lucrece the chaste.

Haply that name of chaste unhappily set   **8**
This bateless edge on his keen appetite;
When Collatine unwisely did not let
To praise the clear unmatched red and white
Which triumph'd in that sky of his delight,   **12**
    Where mortal stars, as bright as heaven's beauties,
    With pure aspects did him peculiar duties.

For he the night before, in Tarquin's tent,
Unlock'd the treasure of his happy state;   **16**
What priceless wealth the heavens had him lent
In the possession of his beauteous mate;
Reck'ning his fortune at such high-proud rate,
    That kings might be espoused to more fame,   **20**
    But king nor peer to such a peerless dame.

O happiness enjoy'd but of a few!
And, if possess'd, as soon decay'd and done
As is the morning's silver-melting dew   **24**
Against the golden splendour of the sun;

---

1 all in post: *with great speed*   3 Lust-breathed: *led by lust*
4 Collatium; *cf. n.*   5 aspire: *ascend*
8, 9 *Cf. n.*   9 bateless: *which cannot be blunted*
10 let: *forbear*   14 aspects; *cf. n.*

An expir'd date, cancell'd ere well begun:
　Honour and beauty, in the owner's arms,
　Are weakly fortress'd from a world of harms.   28

Beauty itself doth of itself persuade
The eyes of men without an orator;
What needeth then apology be made
To set forth that which is so singular?   32
Or why is Collatine the publisher
　Of that rich jewel he should keep unknown
　From thievish ears, because it is his own?

Perchance his boast of Lucrece' sov'reignty   36
Suggested this proud issue of a king;
For by our ears our hearts oft tainted be:
Perchance that envy of so rich a thing,
Braving compare, disdainfully did sting   40
　His high-pitch'd thoughts, that meaner men should
　　vaunt
　That golden hap which their superiors want.

But some untimely thought did instigate
His all-too-timeless speed, if none of those: 44
His honour, his affairs, his friends, his state,
Neglected all, with swift intent he goes
To quench the coal which in his liver glows.
　O rash false heat, wrapp'd in repentant cold!   48
　Thy hasty spring still blasts, and ne'er grows old.

When at Collatium this false lord arriv'd,
Well was he welcom'd by the Roman dame,
Within whose face beauty and virtue striv'd   52
Which of them both should underprop her fame:

26 *Cf. n.*
37 Suggested: *tempted*
49 spring; *cf. n.*

33 publisher: *proclaimer*
47 liver; *cf. n.*
52-70 *Cf. n.*

When virtue bragg'd, beauty would blush for shame;
When beauty boasted blushes, in despite
Virtue would stain that o'er with silver white.   56

But beauty, in that white intituled,
From Venus' doves doth challenge that fair field;
Then virtue claims from beauty beauty's red,
Which virtue gave the golden age to gild   60
Their silver cheeks, and call'd it then their shield;
Teaching them thus to use it in the fight,
When shame assail'd, the red should fence the white.

This heraldry in Lucrece' face was seen,   64
Argu'd by beauty's red and virtue's white:
Of either's colour was the other queen,
Proving from world's minority their right:
Yet their ambition makes them still to fight;   68
The sovereignty of either being so great,
That oft they interchange each other's seat.

This silent war of lilies and of roses,
Which Tarquin view'd in her fair face's field,   72
In their pure ranks his traitor eye encloses;
Where, lest between them both it should be kill'd
The coward captive vanquished doth yield
To those two armies that would let him go,   76
Rather than triumph in so false a foe.

Now thinks he that her husband's shallow tongue—
The niggard prodigal that prais'd her so—
In that high task hath done her beauty wrong,   80
Which far exceeds his barren skill to show:

65 Argu'd: *evinced*   67 minority; *cf. n.*
72 field; *cf. n.*   73 pure: *unmixed*

Therefore that praise which Collatine doth owe
　　Enchanted Tarquin answers with surmise,
　　In silent wonder of still-gazing eyes.　　　　　　84

This earthly saint, adored by this devil,
Little suspecteth the false worshipper;
For unstain'd thoughts do seldom dream on evil,
Birds never lim'd no secret bushes fear:　　　　　　88
So guiltless she securely gives good cheer
　　And reverend welcome to her princely guest,
　　Whose inward ill no outward harm express'd:

For that he colour'd with his high estate,　　　　　　92
Hiding base sin in plaits of majesty;
That nothing in him seem'd inordinate,
Save sometime too much wonder of his eye,
Which, having all, all could not satisfy;　　　　　　96
　　But, poorly rich, so wanteth in his store,
　　That, cloy'd with much, he pineth still for more.

But she, that never cop'd with stranger eyes,
Could pick no meaning from their parling looks,　　100
Nor read the subtle-shining secrecies
Writ in the glassy margents of such books:
She touch'd no unknown baits, nor fear'd no hooks;
　　Nor could she moralize his wanton sight,　　　　104
　　More than his eyes were open'd to the light.

He stories to her ears her husband's fame,
Won in the fields of fruitful Italy;
And decks with praises Collatine's high name,　　　108
Made glorious by his manly chivalry

82 owe; *cf. n.*　　　　　83 Enchanted: *fascinated*　　　answers: *pays*
88 lim'd; *cf. n.*　　　　　　　　　　　　　89 securely: *unsuspectingly*
90 reverend: *reverent*　　　　　　　　　　　　　　　93 plaits: *folds*
99 cop'd with: *encountered*　　　　　　　　　100 parling: *speaking*
102 margents: *margins*　　　　　　　　　104 moralize: *interpret*
104, 105 *Cf. n.*　　　　　　　　　　　　　　106-112 *Cf. n.*

With bruised arms and wreaths of victory:
  Her joy with heav'd-up hand she doth express,
  And, wordless, so greets heaven for his success. 112

Far from the purpose of his coming thither,
He makes excuses for his being there:
No cloudy show of stormy blustering weather
Doth yet in this fair welkin once appear;   116
  Till sable Night, mother of Dread and Fear,
  Upon the world dim darkness doth display,
  And in her vaulty prison stows the Day.

For then is Tarquin brought unto his bed,   120
Intending weariness with heavy spright;
For after supper long he questioned
With modest Lucrece, and wore out the night:
Now leaden slumber with life's strength doth fight, 124
  And every one to rest themselves betake,
  Save thieves, and cares, and troubled minds, that
    wake.

As one of which doth Tarquin lie revolving
The sundry dangers of his will's obtaining;   128
Yet ever to obtain his will resolving,
Though weak-built hopes persuade him to abstaining:
Despair to gain doth traffic oft for gaining;
  And when great treasure is the meed propos'd,   132
  Though death be adjunct, there's no death suppos'd.

Those that much covet are with gain so fond,
That what they have not, that which they possess
They scatter and unloose it from their bond,   136
And so, by hoping more, they have but less;

111 heav'd-up: *uplifted*
117 sable: *black*
121 Intending: *pretending*
135. 136 *Cf. n.*

117-119 *Cf. n.*
120-123 *Cf. n.*
122 questioned: *conversed*

Or, gaining more, the profit of excess
 Is but to surfeit, and such griefs sustain,
 That they prove bankrupt in this poor-rich gain. 140

The aim of all is but to nurse the life
With honour, wealth, and ease, in waning age;
And in this aim there is such thwarting strife,
That one for all, or all for one we gage;   144
As life for honour in fell battles' rage;
 Honour for wealth; and oft that wealth doth cost
 The death of all, and all together lost.

So that in venturing ill we leave to be   148
The things we are for that which we expect;
And this ambitious foul infirmity,
In having much, torments us with defect
Of that we have: so then we do neglect   152
 The thing we have: and, all for want of wit,
 Make something nothing by augmenting it.

Such hazard now must doting Tarquin make,
Pawning his honour to obtain his lust,   156
And for himself himself he must forsake:
Then where is truth, if there be no self-trust?
When shall he think to find a stranger just,
 When he himself himself confounds, betrays 160
 To slanderous tongues and wretched hateful days?

Now stole upon the time the dead of night,
When heavy sleep had clos'd up mortal eyes;
No comfortable star did lend his light,   164
No noise but owls' and wolves' death-boding cries;

138-140 *Cf. n.*   144 gage: *impawn, hazard*
150-152 *Cf. n.*   160 confounds: *overthrows*

Now serves the season that they may surprise
  The silly lambs; pure thoughts are dead and still,
  While lust and murder wake to stain and kill.   168

And now this lustful lord leap'd from his bed,
Throwing his mantle rudely o'er his arm;
Is madly toss'd between desire and dread;
Th' one sweetly flatters, th' other feareth harm;   172
But honest fear, bewitch'd with lust's foul charm,
  Doth too too oft betake him to retire,
  Beaten away by brain-sick rude desire.

His falchion on a flint he softly smiteth,   176
That from the cold stone sparks of fire do fly;
Whereat a waxen torch forthwith he lighteth,
Which must be lode-star to his lustful eye;
And to the flame thus speaks advisedly: 180
  'As from this cold flint I enforc'd this fire,
  So Lucrece must I force to my desire.'

Here pale with fear he doth premeditate
The dangers of his loathsome enterprise,   184
And in his inward mind he doth debate
What following sorrow may on this arise:
Then looking scornfully, he doth despise
  His naked armour of still-slaughter'd lust,   188
  And justly thus controls his thoughts unjust:

'Fair torch, burn out thy light, and lend it not
To darken her whose light excelleth thine;
And die, unhallow'd thoughts, before you blot   192
With your uncleanness that which is divine;

167 silly: *harmless*   174 retire: *retreat*
187, 188 *Cf. n.*

Offer pure incense to so pure a shrine:
  Let fair humanity abhor the deed
  That spots and stains love's modest snow-white
      weed.   196

'O shame to knighthood and to shining arms!
O foul dishonour to my household's grave!
O impious act, including all foul harms!
A martial man to be soft fancy's slave!   200
True valour still a true respect should have;
  Then my digression is so vile, so base,
  That it will live engraven in my face.

'Yea, though I die, the scandal will survive,   204
And be an eye-sore in my golden coat;
Some loathsome dash the herald will contrive,
To cipher me how fondly I did dote;
That my posterity sham'd with the note,   208
  Shall curse my bones, and hold it for no sin
  To wish that I their father had not been.

'What win I if I gain the thing I seek?
A dream, a breath, a froth of fleeting joy.   212
Who buys a minute's mirth to wail a week?
Or sells eternity to get a toy?
For one sweet grape who will the vine destroy?
  Or what fond beggar, but to touch the crown,   216
  Would with the sceptre straight be stroken down?

'If Collatinus dream of my intent,
Will he not wake, and in a desperate rage
Post hither, this vile purpose to prevent?   220
This siege that hath engirt his marriage,

197 weed: *dress*   197-210 *Cf. n.*
 200 fancy's: *love's*   202 digression: *misdeed*
206, 207 *Cf. n.*   207 cipher: *express by a sign*
217 stroken: *struck*

This blur to youth, this sorrow to the sage,
   This dying virtue, this surviving shame,
     Whose crime will bear an ever-during blame?   224

'O, what excuse can my invention make,
When thou shalt charge me with so black a deed?
Will not my tongue be mute, my frail joints shake,
Mine eyes forgo their light, my false heart bleed? 228
The guilt being great, the fear doth still exceed;
   And extreme fear can neither fight nor fly,
     But coward-like with trembling terror die.

'Had Collatinus kill'd my son or sire,   232
Or lain in ambush to betray my life,
Or were he not my dear friend, this desire
Might have excuse to work upon his wife,
As in revenge or quittal of such strife: 236
   But as he is my kinsman, my dear friend,
     The shame and fault finds no excuse nor end.

'Shameful it is; ay, if the fact be known:
Hateful it is; there is no hate in loving: 240
I'll beg her love; but she is not her own:
The worst is but denial and reproving:
My will is strong, past reason's weak removing.
   Who fears a sentence, or an old man's saw,   244
     Shall by a painted cloth be kept in awe.'

Thus, graceless, holds he disputation
'Tween frozen conscience and hot-burning will,
And with good thoughts makes dispensation,   248
Urging the worser sense for vantage still;

236 quittal: *requital*   245 painted cloth; *cf. n.*
248 makes dispensation: *dispenses*   249 vantage: *vantage ground*

Which in a moment doth confound and kill
    All pure effects, and doth so far proceed,
    That what is vile shows like a virtuous deed.   252

Quoth he, 'She took me kindly by the hand,
And gaz'd for tidings in my eager eyes,
Fearing some hard news from the warlike band
Where her beloved Collatinus lies.   256
O how her fear did make her colour rise!
    First red as roses that on lawn we lay,
    Then white as lawn, the roses took away.

'And how her hand, in my hand being lock'd,   260
Forc'd it to tremble with her loyal fear!
Which struck her sad, and then it faster rock'd,
Until her husband's welfare she did hear;
Whereat she smiled with so sweet a cheer,   264
    That had Narcissus seen her as she stood,
    Self-love had never drown'd him in the flood.

'Why hunt I then for colour or excuses?
All orators are dumb when beauty pleadeth;   268
Poor wretches have remorse in poor abuses;
Love thrives not in the heart that shadows dreadeth:
Affection is my captain, and he leadeth;
    And when his gaudy banner is display'd,   272
    The coward fights and will not be dismay'd.

'Then, childish fear, avaunt! debating, die!
Respect and reason, wait on wrinkled age!
My heart shall never countermand mine eye: 276
Sad pause and deep regard beseem the sage;
My part is youth, and beats these from the stage.

Desire my pilot is, beauty my prize;
Then who fears sinking where such treasure
lies?' 280

As corn o'ergrown by weeds, so heedful fear
Is almost chok'd by unresisted lust.
Away he steals with open listening ear,
Full of foul hope, and full of fond mistrust; 284
Both which, as servitors to the unjust,
    So cross him with their opposite persuasion,
    That now he vows a league, and now invasion.

Within his thought her heavenly image sits, 288
And in the self-same seat sits Collatine:
That eye which looks on her confounds his wits;
That eye which him beholds, as more divine,
Unto a view so false will not incline; 292
    But with a pure appeal seeks to the heart,
    Which once corrupted, takes the worser part;

And therein heartens up his servile powers,
Who, flatter'd by their leader's jocund show, 296
Stuff up his lust, as minutes fill up hours;
And as their captain, so their pride doth grow,
Paying more slavish tribute than they owe.
    By reprobate desire thus madly led, 300
    The Roman lord marcheth to Lucrece' bed.

The locks between her chamber and his will,
Each one by him enforc'd, retires his ward;
But as they open they all rate his ill, 304
Which drives the creeping thief to some regard:
The threshold grates the door to have him heard;
    Night-wand'ring weasels shriek to see him there;
    They fright him, yet he still pursues his fear. 308

303 retires: *withdraws*   305 regard: *consideration*

As each unwilling portal yields him way,
Through little vents and crannies of the place
The wind wars with his torch to make him stay,
And blows the smoke of it into his face,   312
Extinguishing his conduct in this case;
   But his hot heart, which fond desire doth scorch,
   Puffs forth another wind that fires the torch:

And being lighted, by the light he spies   316
Lucretia's glove, wherein her needle sticks:
He takes it from the rushes where it lies,
And griping it, the needle his finger pricks;
As who should say, 'This glove to wanton tricks   320
   Is not inur'd; return again in haste;
   Thou seest our mistress' ornaments are chaste.'

But all these poor forbiddings could not stay him;
He in the worst sense construes their denial: 324
The door, the wind, the glove, that did delay him,
He takes for accidental things of trial;
Or as those bars which stop the hourly dial,
   Who with a ling'ring stay his course doth let,   328
   Till every minute pays the hour his debt.

'So, so,' quoth he, 'these lets attend the time,
Like little frosts that sometime threat the spring,
To add a more rejoicing to the prime,   332
And give the sneaped birds more cause to sing.
Pain pays the income of each precious thing;
   Huge rocks, high winds, strong pirates, shelves and
      sands,
   The merchant fears, ere rich at home he lands.' 336

313 conduct: *guide*   318 rushes; *cf. n.*
328 let: *hinder*   332 prime: *spring*
333 sneaped: *pinched with frost*   334 income: *arrival*
335 shelves: *sandbanks*

Now is he come unto the chamber door,
That shuts him from the heaven of his thought,
Which with a yielding latch, and with no more,
Hath barr'd him from the blessed thing he sought. 340
So from himself impiety hath wrought,
    That for his prey to pray he doth begin,
    As if the heavens should countenance his sin.

But in the midst of his unfruitful prayer,   344
Having solicited the eternal power
That his foul thoughts might compass his fair fair,
And they would stand auspicious to the hour,
Even there he starts: quoth he, 'I must deflower;   348
    The powers to whom I pray abhor this fact,
    How can they then assist me in the act?

'Then Love and Fortune be my gods, my guide!
My will is back'd with resolution: 352
Thoughts are but dreams till their effects be tried;
The blackest sin is clear'd with absolution;
Against love's fire fear's frost hath dissolution.
    The eye of heaven is out, and misty night   356
    Covers the shame that follows sweet delight.'

This said, his guilty hand pluck'd up the latch,
And with his knee the door he opens wide.
The dove sleeps fast that this night-owl will catch: 360
Thus treason works ere traitors be espied.
Who sees the lurking serpent steps aside;
    But she, sound sleeping, fearing no such thing,
    Lies at the mercy of his mortal sting.   364

Into the chamber wickedly he stalks,
And gazeth on her yet unstained bed.

341 *Cf. n.*   342 prey, pray; *cf. n.*   349 fact: *misdeed*
356 eye of heaven; *cf. n.*   365 stalks; *cf. n.*

The curtains being close, about he walks,
Rolling his greedy eyeballs in his head: 368
By their high treason is his heart misled;
    Which gives the watchword to his hand full soon,
    To draw the cloud that hides the silver moon.

Look, as the fair and fiery-pointed sun,   372
Rushing from forth a cloud, bereaves our sight;
Even so, the curtain drawn, his eyes begun
To wink, being blinded with a greater light:
Whether it is that she reflects so bright,   376
    That dazzleth them, or else some shame supposed,
    But blind they are, and keep themselves enclosed.

O had they in that darksome prison died,
Then had they seen the period of their ill;   380
Then Collatine again, by Lucrece' side,
In his clear bed might have reposed still:
But they must ope, this blessed league to kill,
    And holy-thoughted Lucrece to their sight   384
    Must sell her joy, her life, her world's delight.

Her lily hand her rosy cheek lies under,
Cozening the pillow of a lawful kiss;
Who, therefore angry, seems to part in sunder,   388
Swelling on either side to want his bliss;
Between whose hills her head entombed is:
    Where, like a virtuous monument she lies,
    To be admir'd of lewd unhallow'd eyes.   392

Without the bed her other fair hand was,
On the green coverlet; whose perfect white
Show'd like an April daisy on the grass,

380 period: *end*   386-395 *Cf. n.*
389 to want: *as if in anger at being deprived of*

With pearly sweat, resembling dew of night.   396
Her eyes, like marigolds, had sheath'd their light,
    And canopied in darkness sweetly lay,
    Till they might open to adorn the day.

Her hair, like golden threads, play'd with her
        breath;   400
O modest wantons! wanton modesty!
Showing life's triumph in the map of death,
And death's dim look in life's mortality:
Each in her sleep themselves so beautify,   404
    As if between them twain there were no strife,
    But that life liv'd in death, and death in life.

Her breasts, like ivory globes circled with blue,
A pair of maiden worlds unconquered,   408
Save of their lord no bearing yoke they knew,
And him by oath they truly honoured.
These worlds in Tarquin new ambition bred;
    Who, like a foul usurper, went about   412
    From this fair throne to heave the owner out.

What could he see but mightily he noted?
What did he note but strongly he desir'd?
What he beheld, on that he firmly doted,   416
And in his will his wilful eye he tir'd.
With more than admiration he admir'd
    Her azure veins, her alablaster skin,
    Her coral lips, her snow-white dimpled chin. 420

As the grim lion fawneth o'er his prey,
Sharp hunger by the conquest satisfied,
So o'er this sleeping soul doth Tarquin stay,

397 marigolds; *cf. n.*
400 golden threads; *cf. n.*
407-409 *Cf. n.*
417 tir'd; *cf. n.*
421 fawneth: *shows delight, as a dog does*
402 map: *picture*
413 heave: *drive*
419 alablaster: *alabaster, white*

His rage of lust by gazing qualified;   424
Slack'd, not suppress'd; for standing by her side,
　His eye, which late this mutiny restrains,
　Unto a greater uproar tempts his veins:

And they, like straggling slaves for pillage fight-
　　ing,   428
Obdurate vassals fell exploits effecting,
In bloody death and ravishment delighting,
Nor children's tears nor mothers' groans respecting,
Swell in their pride, the onset still expecting: 432
　Anon his beating heart, alarum striking,
　Gives the hot charge and bids them do their liking.

His drumming heart cheers up his burning eye,
His eye commends the leading to his hand;   436
His hand, as proud of such a dignity,
Smoking with pride, march'd on to make his stand
On her bare breast, the heart of all her land;
　Whose ranks of blue veins, as his hand did scale, 440
　Left their round turrets destitute and pale.

They, mustering to the quiet cabinet
Where their dear governess and lady lies,
Do tell her she is dreadfully beset,   444
And fright her with confusion of their cries:
She, much amaz'd, breaks ope her lock'd-up eyes,
　Who, peeping forth this tumult to behold,
　Are by his flaming torch dimm'd and controll'd. 448

Imagine her as one in dead of night
From forth dull sleep by dreadful fancy waking,
That thinks she hath beheld some ghastly sprite,
Whose grim aspect sets every joint a-shaking;   452

424 qualified: *abated*   436 commends: *entrusts*
437-439 *Cf. n.*   442 cabinet: *closet*

What terror 'tis! but she, in worser taking,
　From sleep disturbed, heedfully doth view
　The sight which makes supposed terror true.

Wrapp'd and confounded in a thousand fears,　456
Like to a new-kill'd bird she trembling lies;
She dares not look; yet, winking, there appears
Quick-shifting antics, ugly in her eyes:
Such shadows are the weak brain's forgeries;　460
　Who, angry that the eyes fly from their lights,
　In darkness daunts them with more dreadful sights.

His hand, that yet remains upon her breast,
Rude ram to batter such an ivory wall!　464
May feel her heart,—poor citizen,—distress'd,
Wounding itself to death, rise up and fall,
Beating her bulk, that his hand shakes withal.
　This moves in him more rage, and lesser pity,　468
　To make the breach and enter this sweet city.

First, like a trumpet, doth his tongue begin
To sound a parley to his heartless foe;
Who o'er the white sheet peers her whiter chin,　472
The reason of this rash alarm to know,
Which he by dumb demeanour seeks to show;
　But she with vehement prayers urgeth still
　Under what colour he commits this ill.　476

Thus he replies: 'The colour in thy face,—
That even for anger makes the lily pale,
And the red rose blush at her own disgrace,—
Shall plead for me and tell my loving tale;　480

453 taking: *plight*　　　　　　　　　　459 antics; *cf. n.*
467 bulk: *frame*　　　　　　　　　　471 heartless: *timid*
472 peers: *makes to peep out*　　476, 477, 481 colour; *cf. n.*
477-504 *Cf. n.*　　　　　　　　　　477-511 *Cf. n.*

Under that colour am I come to scale
   Thy never-conquer'd fort: the fault is thine,
   For those thine eyes betray thee unto mine.

'Thus I forestall thee, if thou mean to chide: 484
Thy beauty hath ensnar'd thee to this night,
Where thou with patience must my will abide,
My will that marks thee for my earth's delight,
Which I to conquer sought with all my might;   488
   But as reproof and reason beat it dead,
   By thy bright beauty was it newly bred.

'I see what crosses my attempt will bring;
I know what thorns the growing rose defends;   492
I think the honey guarded with a sting;
All this, beforehand, counsel comprehends:
But will is deaf and hears no heedful friends;
   Only he hath an eye to gaze on beauty,   496
   And dotes on what he looks, 'gainst law or duty.

'I have debated, even in my soul,
What wrong, what shame, what sorrow I shall breed;
But nothing can affection's course control,   500
Or stop the headlong fury of his speed.
I know repentant tears ensue the deed,
   Reproach, disdain, and deadly enmity;
   Yet strive I to embrace mine infamy.'   504

This said, he shakes aloft his Roman blade,
Which like a falcon, towering in the skies,
Coucheth the fowl below with his wings' shade,
Whose crooked beak threats if he mount he dies: 508
So under his insulting falchion lies
   Harmless Lucretia, marking what he tells
   With trembling fear, as fowl hear falcon's bells.

492 *Cf. n.*   500 affection: *passion*   507 Coucheth: *causes to crouch*
509 falchion: *sword; cf. n.*   511 falcon's bells; *cf. n.*

'Lucrece,' quoth he, 'this night I must enjoy thee: 512
If thou deny, then force must work my way,
For in thy bed I purpose to destroy thee:
That done, some worthless slave of thine I'll slay,
To kill thine honour with thy life's decay;   516
    And in thy dead arms do I mean to place him,
    Swearing I slew him, seeing thee embrace him.

'So thy surviving husband shall remain
The scornful mark of every open eye;   520
Thy kinsmen hang their heads at this disdain,
Thy issue blurr'd with nameless bastardy:
And thou, the author of their obloquy,
    Shalt have thy trespass cited up in rimes,   524
    And sung by children in succeeding times.

'But if thou yield, I rest thy secret friend:
The fault unknown is as a thought unacted;
A little harm done to a great good end,   528
For lawful policy remains enacted.
The poisonous simple sometimes is compacted
    In a pure compound; being so applied,
    His venom in effect is purified.   532

'Then for thy husband and thy children's sake,
Tender my suit: bequeath not to their lot
The shame that from them no device can take,
The blemish that will never be forgot;   536
Worse than a slavish wipe or birth-hour's blot:
    For marks descried in men's nativity
    Are nature's faults, not their own infamy.'

Here with a cockatrice' dead-killing eye   540
He rouseth up himself, and makes a pause;

522 nameless bastardy; *cf. n.*   534 Tender: *receive favorably*
537 Worse . . . wipe; *cf. n.*   540 cockatrice; *cf. n.*

While she, the picture of pure piety,
Like a white hind under the gripe's sharp claws,
Pleads in a wilderness where are no laws,   544
 To the rough beast that knows no gentle right,
 Nor aught obeys but his foul appetite.

But when a black-fac'd cloud the world doth threat,
In his dim mist the aspiring mountains hiding,   548
From earth's dark womb some gentle gust doth get,
Which blows these pitchy vapours from their biding,
Hindering their present fall by this dividing;
 So his unhallow'd haste her words delays,   552
 And moody Pluto winks while Orpheus plays.

Yet, foul night-waking cat, he doth but dally,
While in his hold-fast foot the weak mouse panteth:
Her sad behaviour feeds his vulture folly,   556
A swallowing gulf that even in plenty wanteth:
His ear her prayers admits, but his heart granteth
 No penetrable entrance to her plaining:
 Tears harden lust though marble wear with rain-
  ing.   560

Her pity-pleading eyes are sadly fix'd
In the remorseless wrinkles of his face;
Her modest eloquence with sighs is mix'd,
Which to her oratory adds more grace.   564
She puts the period often from his place;
 And midst the sentence so her accent breaks,
 That twice she doth begin ere once she speaks.

She conjures him by high almighty Jove,   568
By knighthood, gentry, and sweet friendship's oath,
By her untimely tears, her husband's love,

543 gripe: *vulture*   556 vulture folly; *cf. n-*
559 plaining: *complaint*   565-567 *Cf. n.*

By holy human law, and common troth,
By heaven and earth, and all the power of both,   572
  That to his borrow'd bed he make retire,
  And stoop to honour, not to foul desire.

Quoth she, 'Reward not hospitality
With such black payment as thou hast pretended;   576
Mud not the fountain that gave drink to thee;
Mar not the thing that cannot be amended;
End thy ill aim before thy shoot be ended;
  He is no woodman that doth bend his bow   580
  To strike a poor unseasonable doe.

'My husband is thy friend, for his sake spare me;
Thyself art mighty, for thine own sake leave me;
Myself a weakling, do not, then, ensnare me;   584
Thou look'st not like deceit, do not deceive me.
My sighs, like whirlwinds, labour hence to heave thee;
  If ever man were mov'd with woman's moans,
  Be moved with my tears, my sighs, my groans.   588

'All which together, like a troubled ocean,
Beat at thy rocky and wrack-threat'ning heart,
To soften it with their continual motion;
For stones dissolv'd to water do convert.   592
O, if no harder than a stone thou art,
  Melt at my tears, and be compassionate!
  Soft pity enters at an iron gate.

'In Tarquin's likeness I did entertain thee;   596
Hast thou put on his shape to do him shame?
To all the host of heaven I complain me,
Thou wrong'st his honour, wound'st his princely name.

576 pretended: *intended*   580 woodman: *hunter*
586 heave: *drive*   592 convert: *change*
596-630 *Cf.* ⋆.

Thou art not what thou seem'st; and if the same,　600
　　Thou seem'st not what thou art, a god, a king;
　　For kings like gods should govern everything.

'How will thy shame be seeded in thine age,
When thus thy vices bud before thy spring!　604
If in thy hope thou dar'st do such outrage,
What dar'st thou not when once thou art a king?
O be rememb'red, no outrageous thing
　　From vassal actors can be wip'd away;　608
　　Then kings' misdeeds cannot be hid in clay.

'This deed will make thee only lov'd for fear;
But happy monarchs still are fear'd for love:
With foul offenders thou perforce must bear,　612
When they in thee the like offences prove:
If but for fear of this, thy will remove;
　　For princes are the glass, the school, the book,
　　Where subjects' eyes do learn, do read, do look.　616

'And wilt thou be the school where Lust shall learn?
Must he in thee read lectures of such shame?
Wilt thou be glass wherein it shall discern
Authority for sin, warrant for blame,　620
To privilege dishonour in thy name?
　　Thou back'st reproach against long-living laud,
　　And mak'st fair reputation but a bawd.

'Hast thou command? by him that gave it thee,　624
From a pure heart command thy rebel will:
Draw not thy sword to guard iniquity,
For it was lent thee all that brood to kill.

603 be seeded: *grow to maturity*
605 in thy hope: *while only an heir*
608 From vassal actors: *done by vassals*

Thy princely office how canst thou fulfil, 628
  When, pattern'd by thy fault, foul sin may say,
  He learn'd to sin, and thou didst teach the way?

'Think but how vile a spectacle it were,
To view thy present trespass in another. 632
Men's faults do seldom to themselves appear;
Their own transgressions partially they smother:
This guilt would seem death-worthy in thy brother.
  O how are they wrapp'd in with infamies 636
  That from their own misdeeds askance their eyes!

'To thee, to thee, my heav'd-up hands appeal,
Not to seducing lust, thy rash relier:
I sue for exil'd majesty's repeal; 640
Let him return, and flattering thoughts retire:
His true respect will prison false desire,
  And wipe the dim mist from thy doting eyne,
  That thou shalt see thy state and pity mine.' 644

'Have done,' quoth he; 'my uncontrolled tide
Turns not, but swells the higher by this let.
Small lights are soon blown out, huge fires abide,
And with the wind in greater fury fret: 648
The petty streams that pay a daily debt
  To their salt sovereign, with their fresh falls' haste
  Add to his flow, but alter not his taste.'

'Thou art,' quoth she, 'a sea, a sovereign king; 652
And lo! there falls into thy boundless flood
Black lust, dishonour, shame, misgoverning,
Who seek to stain the ocean of thy blood.

629 pattern'd by thy fault: *having thy fault as an example*
637 askance: *turn aside*   639 relier: *ally*
640 repeal: *recall from exile*   646 let: *obstacle*

If all these petty ills shall change thy good,   656
   Thy sea within a puddle's womb is hears'd,
   And not the puddle in thy sea dispers'd.

'So shall these slaves be king, and thou their slave;
Thou nobly base, they basely dignified;   660
Thou their fair life, and they thy fouler grave;
Thou loathed in their shame, they in thy pride:
The lesser thing should not the greater hide;
   The cedar stoops not to the base shrub's foot,   664
   But low shrubs wither at the cedar's root.

'So let thy thoughts, low vassals to thy state'—
'No more,' quoth he; 'by heaven, I will not hear thee:
Yield to my love; if not, enforced hate,   668
Instead of love's coy touch, shall rudely tear thee;
That done, despitefully I mean to bear thee
   Unto the base bed of some rascal groom,
   To be thy partner in this shameful doom.'   672

This said, he sets his foot upon the light,
For light and lust are deadly enemies:
Shame folded up in blind concealing night,
When most unseen, then most doth tyrannize.   676
The wolf hath seiz'd his prey, the poor lamb cries;
   Till with her own white fleece her voice controll'd
   Entombs her outcry in her lips' sweet fold:

For with the nightly linen that she wears   680
He pens her piteous clamours in her head,
Cooling his hot face in the chastest tears
That ever modest eyes with sorrow shed.
O that prone lust should stain so pure a bed!   684
   The spots whereof could weeping purify,
   Her tears should drop on them perpetually.

677 *Cf. n.*

But she hath lost a dearer thing than life,
And he hath won what he would lose again; 688
This forced league doth force a further strife;
This momentary joy breeds months of pain;
This hot desire converts to cold disdain:
  Pure Chastity is rifled of her store, 692
  And Lust, the thief, far poorer than before.

Look! as the full-fed hound or gorged hawk,
Unapt for tender smell or speedy flight,
Make slow pursuit, or altogether balk 696
The prey wherein by nature they delight;
So surfeit-taking Tarquin fares this night:
  His taste delicious, in digestion souring,
  Devours his will, that liv'd by foul devouring. 700

O deeper sin than bottomless conceit
Can comprehend in still imagination!
Drunken Desire must vomit his receipt,
Ere he can see his own abomination. 704
While Lust is in his pride, no exclamation
  Can curb his heat, or rein his rash desire,
  Till like a jade Self-will himself doth tire.

And then with lank and lean discolour'd cheek, 708
With heavy eye, knit brow, and strengthless pace,
Feeble Desire, all recreant, poor, and meek,
Like to a bankrupt beggar wails his case:
The flesh being proud, Desire doth fight with
    Grace, 712
  For there it revels; and when that decays,
  The guilty rebel for remission prays.

696 balk: *forsake*
703 receipt; *cf. n.*
714 remission: *pardon*

701 conceit: *imagination*
710 recreant: *cowardly*

So fares it with this faultful lord of Rome,
Who this accomplishment so hotly chas'd;   716
For now against himself he sounds this doom,
That through the length of times he stands disgrac'd;
Besides, his soul's fair temple is defac'd;
    To whose weak ruins muster troops of cares,   720
    To ask the spotted princess how she fares.

She says, her subjects with foul insurrection
Have batter'd down her consecrated wall,
And by their mortal fault brought in subjection   724
Her immortality, and made her thrall
To living death, and pain perpetual:
    Which in her prescience she controlled still,
    But her foresight could not forestall their will.   728

Even in this thought through the dark night he steal-
    eth,
A captive victor that hath lost in gain;
Bearing away the wound that nothing healeth,
The scar that will despite of cure remain;   732
Leaving his spoil perplex'd in greater pain.
    She bears the load of lust he left behind,
    And he the burthen of a guilty mind.

He like a thievish dog creeps sadly thence,   736
She like a wearied lamb lies panting there;
He scowls and hates himself for his offence,
She desperate with her nails her flesh doth tear;
He faintly flies, sweating with guilty fear,   740
    She stays, exclaiming on the direful night;
    He runs, and chides his vanish'd, loath'd delight.

721 princess: *i.e. Tarquin's soul*
733 his spoil: *her whom he has violated*
741 exclaiming on: *crying out against*

He thence departs a heavy convertite,
She there remains a hopeless castaway;   744
He in his speed looks for the morning light,
She prays she never may behold the day;
'For day,' quoth she, 'night's scapes doth open lay,
    And my true eyes have never practis'd how   748
    To cloak offences with a cunning brow.

'They think not but that every eye can see
The same disgrace which they themselves behold;
And therefore would they still in darkness be,   752
To have their unseen sin remain untold;
For they their guilt with weeping will unfold,
    And grave, like water that doth eat in steel,
    Upon my cheeks what helpless shame I feel.'   756

Here she exclaims against repose and rest,
And bids her eyes hereafter still be blind.
She wakes her heart by beating on her breast,
And bids it leap from thence where it may find   760
Some purer chest to close so pure a mind.
    Frantic with grief thus breathes she forth her spite
    Against the unseen secrecy of night:

'O comfort-killing Night, image of hell!   764
Dim register and notary of shame!
Black stage for tragedies and murders fell!
Vast sin-concealing chaos! nurse of blame!
Blind muffled bawd! dark harbour for defame!   768
    Grim cave of death! whispering conspirator
    With close-tongu'd treason and the ravisher!

'O hateful, vaporous, and foggy Night!
Since thou art guilty of my cureless crime,   772

743 convertite: *convert*
755 grave: *engrave*
766 Black stage; *cf. n.*
772 my . . . crime: *the inexpiable crime I suffer*
747 scapes: *wanton acts*
761 close: *enclose*
768 defame: *dishonor*

Muster thy mists to meet the eastern light,
Make war against proportion'd course of time;
Or if thou wilt permit the sun to climb
    His wonted height, yet ere he go to bed,   776
    Knit poisonous clouds about his golden head.

'With rotten damps ravish the morning air;
Let their exhal'd unwholesome breaths make sick
The life of purity, the supreme fair,   780
Ere he arrive his weary noontide prick;
And let thy misty vapours march so thick,
    That in their smoky ranks his smother'd light
    May set at noon and make perpetual night.   784

'Were Tarquin Night, as he is but Night's child,
The silver-shining queen he would distain;
Her twinkling handmaids too, by him defil'd,
Through Night's black bosom should not peep
    again: 788
So should I have co-partners in my pain;
    And fellowship in woe doth woe assuage,
    As palmers' chat makes short their pilgrimage.

'Where now I have no one to blush with me,   792
To cross their arms and hang their heads with mine,
To mask their brows and hide their infamy;
But I alone alone must sit and pine,
Seasoning the earth with showers of silver brine,   796
    Mingling my talk with tears, my grief with groans,
    Poor wasting monuments of lasting moans.

'O Night! thou furnace of foul-reeking smoke,
Let not the jealous Day behold that face   800
Which underneath thy black all-hiding cloak

774 proportion'd: *regulated*
780 fair: *beauty*   781 arrive: *reach*   778 ravish: *deflower*
786 distain: *blot*   prick: *point, mark*

Immodestly lies martyr'd with disgrace:
Keep still possession of thy gloomy place,
   That all the faults which in thy reign are made 804
   May likewise be sepulchred in thy shade.

'Make me not object to the tell-tale Day!
The light will show, character'd in my brow,
The story of sweet chastity's decay,   808
The impious breach of holy wedlock vow:
Yea, the illiterate, that know not how
   To cipher what is writ in learned books,
   Will cote my loathsome trespass in my looks.   812

'The nurse, to still her child, will tell my story,
And fright her crying babe with Tarquin's name;
The orator, to deck his oratory,
Will couple my reproach to Tarquin's shame;   816
Feast-finding minstrels, tuning my defame,
   Will tie the hearers to attend each line,
   How Tarquin wronged me, I Collatine.

'Let my good name, that senseless reputation,   820
For Collatine's dear love be kept unspotted:
If that be made a theme for disputation,
The branches of another root are rotted,
And undeserv'd reproach to him allotted   824
   That is as clear from this attaint of mine,
   As I ere this was pure to Collatine.

'O unseen shame! invisible disgrace!
O unfelt sore! crest-wounding, private scar!   828
Reproach is stamp'd in Collatinus' face,
And Tarquin's eye may read the mot afar,

807 character'd: *inscribed*
812 cote: *note, quote*
828 crest-wounding; *cf. n.*

811 cipher: *decipher*
825 attaint: *wound to honor*
830 mot; *cf. n.*

How he in peace is wounded, not in war.
 Alas! how many bear such shameful blows, 832
 Which not themselves, but he that gives them knows.

'If, Collatine, thine honour lay in me,
From me by strong assault it is bereft.
My honey lost, and I, a drone-like bee, 836
Have no perfection of my summer left,
But robb'd and ransack'd by injurious theft:
 In thy weak hive a wandering wasp hath crept,
 And suck'd the honey which thy chaste bee kept. 840

'Yet am I guilty of thy honour's wrack;
Yet for thy honour did I entertain him;
Coming from thee, I could not put him back,
For it had been dishonour to disdain him: 844
Besides, of weariness he did complain him,
 And talk'd of virtue: O unlook'd-for evil,
 When virtue is profan'd in such a devil!

'Why should the worm intrude the maiden bud? 848
Or hateful cuckoos hatch in sparrows' nests?
Or toads infect fair founts with venom mud?
Or tyrant folly lurk in gentle breasts?
Or kings be breakers of their own behests? 852
 But no perfection is so absolute,
 That some impurity doth not pollute.

'The aged man that coffers-up his gold
Is plagu'd with cramps and gouts and painful fits; 856
And scarce hath eyes his treasure to behold,
But like still-pining Tantalus he sits,
And useless barns the harvest of his wits;
 Having no other pleasure of his gain 860
 But torment that it cannot cure his pain.

---

848 intrude: *invade*
858 Tantalus; *cf. n.*
      850 toads infect; *cf. n.*
      859 barns: *lays up in a barn*

'So then he hath it when he cannot use it,
And leaves it to be master'd by his young;
Who in their pride do presently abuse it: 864
Their father was too weak, and they too strong,
To hold their cursed-blessed fortune long.
   The sweets we wish for turn to loathed sours
   Even in the moment that we call them ours.   868

'Unruly blasts wait on the tender spring;
Unwholesome weeds take root with precious flowers;
The adder hisses where the sweet birds sing;
What virtue breeds iniquity devours: 872
We have no good that we can say is ours,
   But ill-annexed Opportunity
   Or kills his life, or else his quality.

'O Opportunity! thy guilt is great,   876
'Tis thou that execut'st the traitor's treason;
Thou sett'st the wolf where he the lamb may get;
Whoever plots the sin, thou point'st the season;
'Tis thou that spurn'st at right, at law, at reason; 880
   And in thy shady cell, where none may spy him,
   Sits Sin to seize the souls that wander by him.

'Thou mak'st the vestal violate her oath;
Thou blow'st the fire when temperance is thaw'd; 884
Thou smother'st honesty, thou murth'rest troth;
Thou foul abettor! thou notorious bawd!
Thou plantest scandal and displacest laud:
   Thou ravisher, thou traitor, thou false thief, 888
   Thy honey turns to gall, thy joy to grief!

'Thy secret pleasure turns to open shame,
Thy private feasting to a public fast,

874 ill-annexed; *cf. n.*   875 Or: *either*
876, etc. *Cf. n.*   879 point'st: *appointest*

Thy smoothing titles to a ragged name,   892
Thy sugar'd tongue to bitter wormwood taste:
Thy violent vanities can never last.
    How comes it, then, vile Opportunity,
    Being so bad, such numbers seek for thee?   896

'When wilt thou be the humble suppliant's friend,
And bring him where his suit may be obtain'd?
When wilt thou sort an hour great strifes to end?
Or free that soul which wretchedness hath chain'd? 900
Give physic to the sick, ease to the pain'd?
    The poor, lame, blind, halt, creep, cry out for thee;
    But they ne'er meet with Opportunity.

'The patient dies while the physician sleeps;   904
The orphan pines while the oppressor feeds;
Justice is feasting while the widow weeps;
Advice is sporting while infection breeds:
Thou grant'st no time for charitable deeds: 908
    Wrath, envy, treason, rape, and murther's rages,
    Thy heinous hours wait on them as their pages.

'When Truth and Virtue have to do with thee,
A thousand crosses keep them from thy aid: 912
They buy thy help; but Sin ne'er gives a fee,
He gratis comes; and thou art well appaid
As well to hear as grant what he hath said.
    My Collatine would else have come to me   916
    When Tarquin did, but he was stay'd by thee.

'Guilty thou art of murther and of theft,
Guilty of perjury and subornation,
Guilty of treason, forgery, and shift,   920

892 smoothing: *flattering*   899 sort: *choose*
905 pines: *hungers*   914 appaid: *satisfied*
920 shift: *stratagem*

Guilty of incest, that abomination;
An accessary by thine inclination
  To all sins past, and all that are to come,
  From the creation to the general doom.   924

'Misshapen Time, copesmate of ugly Night,
Swift subtle post, carrier of grisly care,
Eater of youth, false slave to false delight,
Base watch of woes, sin's pack-horse, virtue's
    snare;   928
Thou nursest all, and murthrest all that are;
  O hear me, then, injurious, shifting Time!
  Be guilty of my death, since of my crime.

'Why hath thy servant, Opportunity,   932
Betray'd the hours thou gav'st me to repose?
Cancell'd my fortunes, and enchained me
To endless date of never-ending woes?
Time's office is to fine the hate of foes;   936
  To eat up errors by opinion bred,
  Not spend the dowry of a lawful bed.

'Time's glory is to calm contending kings,
To unmask falsehood and bring truth to light,   940
To stamp the seal of time in aged things,
To wake the morn and sentinel the night,
To wrong the wronger till he render right,
  To ruinate proud buildings with thy hours,   944
  And smear with dust their glittering golden towers;

'To fill with worm-holes stately monuments,
To feed oblivion with decay of things,
To blot old books and alter their contents,   948
To pluck the quills from ancient ravens' wings,

To dry the old oak's sap and cherish springs,
   To spoil antiquities of hammer'd steel,
   And turn the giddy round of Fortune's wheel;   952

'To show the beldam daughters of her daughter,
To make the child a man, the man a child,
To slay the tiger that doth live by slaughter,
To tame the unicorn and lion wild,   956
To mock the subtle, in themselves beguil'd,
   To cheer the ploughman with increaseful crops,
   And waste huge stones with little water-drops.

'Why work'st thou mischief in thy pilgrimage,   960
Unless thou couldst return to make amends?
One poor retiring minute in an age
Would purchase thee a thousand thousand friends,
Lending him wit that to bad debtors lends: 964
   O, this dread night, wouldst thou one hour come
     back,
   I could prevent this storm and shun thy wrack.

'Thou ceaseless lackey to eternity,
With some mischance cross Tarquin in his flight: 968
Devise extremes beyond extremity,
To make him curse this cursed crimeful night:
Let ghastly shadows his lewd eyes affright,
   And the dire thought of his committed evil   972
   Shape every bush a hideous shapeless devil.

'Disturb his hours of rest with restless trances,
Afflict him in his bed with bedrid groans;
Let there bechance him pitiful mischances   976
To make him moan, but pity not his moans;

950 cherish; *cf. n.*
956 unicorn; *cf. n.*

953 beldam: *grandmother*
962 retiring: *returning*

Stone him with harden'd hearts, harder than stones;
   And let mild women to him lose their mildness,
     Wilder to him than tigers in their wildness.   980

'Let him have time to tear his curled hair,
Let him have time against himself to rave,
Let him have time of Time's help to despair,
Let him have time to live a loathed slave,   984
Let him have time a beggar's orts to crave,
   And time to see one that by alms doth live
   Disdain to him disdained scraps to give.

'Let him have time to see his friends his foes,   988
And merry fools to mock at him resort;
Let him have time to mark how slow time goes
In time of sorrow, and how swift and short
His time of folly and his time of sport;   992
   And ever let his unrecalling crime
   Have time to wail the abusing of his time.

'O Time! thou tutor both to good and bad,
Teach me to curse him that thou taught'st this ill; 996
At his own shadow let the thief run mad,
Himself himself seek every hour to kill:
Such wretched hands such wretched blood should spill;
   For who so base would such an office have   1000
   As slanderous deathsman to so base a slave?

'The baser is he, coming from a king,
To shame his hope with deeds degenerate:
The mightier man, the mightier is the thing   1004
That makes him honour'd, or begets him hate;
For greatest scandal waits on greatest state.
   The moon being clouded presently is miss'd,
   But little stars may hide them when they list.   1008

985 orts: *refuse*   993 unrecalling: *irrevocable*
1001 slanderous: *contemptible*   deathsman: *executioner*

'The crow may bathe his coal-black wings in mire,
And unperceiv'd fly with the filth away;
But if the like the snow-white swan desire,
The stain upon his silver down will stay.   1012
Poor grooms are sightless night, kings glorious day.
    Gnats are unnoted wheresoe'er they fly,
    But eagles gaz'd upon with every eye.

'Out, idle words! servants to shallow fools,   1016
Unprofitable sounds, weak arbitrators!
Busy yourselves in skill-contending schools;
Debate where leisure serves with dull debaters;
To trembling clients be you mediators: 1020
    For me, I force not argument a straw,
    Since that my case is past the help of law.

'In vain I rail at Opportunity,
At Time, at Tarquin, and uncheerful Night;   1024
In vain I cavil with my infamy,
In vain I spurn at my confirm'd despite;
This helpless smoke of words doth me no right.
    The remedy indeed to do me good,   1028
    Is to let forth my foul defiled blood.

'Poor hand, why quiver'st thou at this decree?
Honour thyself to rid me of this shame;
For if I die, my honour lives in thee,   1032
But if I live, thou liv'st in my defame;
Since thou couldst not defend thy loyal dame,
    And wast afeard to scratch her wicked foe,
    Kill both thyself and her for yielding so.'   1036

This said, from her be-tumbled couch she starteth,
To find some desperate instrument of death;

1013 grooms: *fellows*   1021 force: *care for*
1037 be-tumbled: *disordered*

But this no slaughter-house no tool imparteth
To make more vent for passage of her breath; 1040
Which, thronging through her lips, so vanisheth
　　As smoke from Ætna, that in air consumes,
　　Or that which from discharged cannon fumes.

'In vain,' quoth she, 'I live, and seek in vain 1044
Some happy mean to end a hapless life:
I fear'd by Tarquin's falchion to be slain,
Yet for the self-same purpose seek a knife:
But when I fear'd I was a loyal wife: 1048
　　So am I now: O no! that cannot be;
　　Of that true type hath Tarquin rifled me.

'O that is gone for which I sought to live!
And therefore now I need not fear to die. 1052
To clear this spot by death, at least I give
A badge of fame to slander's livery;
A dying life to living infamy.
　　Poor helpless help, the treasure stol'n away, 1056
　　To burn the guiltless casket where it lay?

'Well, well, dear Collatine, thou shalt not know
The stained taste of violated troth;
I will not wrong thy true affection so, 1060
To flatter thee with an infringed oath;
This bastard graff shall never come to growth;
　　He shall not boast who did thy stock pollute
　　That thou art doting father of his fruit. 1064

'Nor shall he smile at thee in secret thought,
Nor laugh with his companions at thy state;
But thou shalt know thy interest was not bought
Basely with gold, but stol'n from forth thy gate. 1068

1054 badge, livery; *cf. n.*　　　　　　1062 graff: *graft*
1067 interest: *property*

For me, I am the mistress of my fate,
   And with my trespass never will dispense,
   Till life to death acquit my forc'd offence.

'I will not poison thee with my attaint,   1072
Nor fold my fault in cleanly-coin'd excuses;
My sable ground of sin I will not paint,
To hide the truth of this false night's abuses;
My tongue shall utter all; mine eyes, like sluices, 1076
   As from a mountain-spring that feeds a dale,
   Shall gush pure streams to purge my impure tale.'

By this, lamenting Philomel had ended
The well-tun'd warble of her nightly sorrow,   1080
And solemn night with slow sad gait descended
To ugly hell; when, lo! the blushing morrow
Lends light to all fair eyes that light will borrow:
   But cloudy Lucrece shames herself to see,   1084
   And therefore still in night would cloister'd be.

Revealing day through every cranny spies,
And seems to point her out where she sits weeping;
To whom she sobbing speaks: 'O eye of eyes!   1088
Why pry'st thou through my window? leave thy peep-
    ing;
Mock with thy tickling beams eyes that are sleeping:
   Brand not my forehead with thy piercing light,
   For day hath naught to do what's done by
    night.'   1092

Thus cavils she with everything she sees:
True grief is fond and testy as a child,
Who wayward once, his mood with nought agrees:
Old woes, not infant sorrows, bear them mild;   1096

1070 dispense: *put up*   1074 sable ground; *cf. n.*
1079 Philomel; *cf. n.*   1086 *Cf. n.*   1094 *Cf. n.*

Continuance tames the one; the other wild,
  Like an unpractis'd swimmer plunging still,
  With too much labour drowns for want of skill.

So she, deep-drenched in a sea of care,   1100
Holds disputation with each thing she views,
And to herself all sorrow doth compare;
No object but her passion's strength renews,
And as one shifts, another straight ensues: 1104
  Sometime her grief is dumb and hath no words;
  Sometime 'tis mad and too much talk affords.

The little birds that tune their morning's joy
Make her moans mad with their sweet melody: 1108
For mirth doth search the bottom of annoy;
Sad souls are slain in merry company;
Grief best is pleas'd with grief's society:
  True sorrow then is feelingly suffic'd   1112
  When with like semblance it is sympathiz'd.

'Tis double death to drown in ken of shore;
He ten times pines that pines beholding food;
To see the salve doth make the wound ache more; 1116
Great grief grieves most at that would do it good;
Deep woes roll forward like a gentle flood,
  Who, being stopp'd, the bounding banks o'erflows;
  Grief dallied with nor law nor limit knows.   1120

'You mocking birds,' quoth she, 'your tunes entomb
Within your hollow-swelling feather'd breasts,
And in my hearing be you mute and dumb:
My restless discord loves no stops nor rests;   1124
A woeful hostess brooks not merry guests:
  Relish your nimble notes to pleasing ears;
  Distress likes dumps when time is kept with tears.

1114 ken: *view*   1120 dallied: *trifled*
1126 Relish: *sing*   1127 dumps: *doleful ditties*

'Come, Philomel, that sing'st of ravishment,   1128
Make thy sad grove in my dishevell'd hair:
As the dank earth weeps at thy languishment,
So I at each sad strain will strain a tear,
And with deep groans the diapason bear;   1132
    For burthen-wise I'll hum on Tarquin still,
    While thou on Tereus descant'st better skill.

'And whiles against a thorn thou bear'st thy part
To keep thy sharp woes waking, wretched I,   1136
To imitate thee well, against my heart
Will fix a sharp knife to affright mine eye,
Who, if it wink, shall thereon fall and die.
    These means, as frets upon an instrument,   1140
    Shall tune our heart-strings to true languishment.

'And for, poor bird, thou sing'st not in the day,
As shaming any eye should thee behold,
Some dark deep desert, seated from the way,   1144
That knows not parching heat nor freezing cold,
We will find out; and there we will unfold
    To creatures stern sad tunes, to change their kinds:
    Since men prove beasts, let beasts bear gentle
        minds.'   1148

As the poor frighted deer, that stands at gaze,
Wildly determining which way to fly,
Or one encompass'd with a winding maze,
That cannot tread the way out readily;   1152
So with herself is she in mutiny,
    To live or die which of the twain were better,
    When life is sham'd, and death reproach's debtor.

1130 dank: *damp*   1132 diapason; *cf. n.*
1133 burthen; *cf. n.*
1134 Tereus; *cf. note on 1079*   descant'st; *cf. n.*   better skill; *cf. n.*
1139 *Cf. n.*   1140 frets; *cf. n.*
1143 shaming: *being ashamed*   1155 death reproach's debtor; *cf. n.*

'To kill myself,' quoth she, 'alack! what were it   1156
But with my body my poor soul's pollution?
They that lose half with greater patience bear it
Than they whose whole is swallow'd in confusion.
That mother tries a merciless conclusion,   1160
   Who, having two sweet babes, when death takes
     one,
   Will slay the other and be nurse to none.

'My body or my soul, which was the dearer,
When the one, pure, the other made divine?   1164
Whose love of either to myself was nearer,
When both were kept for heaven and Collatine?
Ay me! the bark peel'd from the lofty pine,
   His leaves will wither and his sap decay;   1168
   So must my soul, her bark being peel'd away.

'Her house is sack'd, her quiet interrupted,
Her mansion batter'd by the enemy;
Her sacred temple spotted, spoil'd, corrupted,   1172
Grossly engirt with daring infamy:
Then let it not be call'd impiety,
   If in this blemish'd fort I make some hole
   Through which I may convey this troubled soul. 1176

'Yet die I will not till my Collatine
Have heard the cause of my untimely death;
That he may vow, in that sad hour of mine,
Revenge on him that made me stop my breath.   1180
My stained blood to Tarquin I'll bequeath,
   Which by him tainted, shall for him be spent,
   And as his due writ in my testament.

'Mine honour I'll bequeath unto the knife   1184
That wounds my body so dishonoured.

1157 *Cf. n.*   1160 conclusion: *experiment*

'Tis honour to deprive dishonour'd life;
The one will live, the other being dead:
So of shame's ashes shall my fame be bred;   1188
   For in my death I murther shameful scorn:
   My shame so dead, mine honour is new-born.

'Dear lord of that dear jewel I have lost,
What legacy shall I bequeath to thee?   1192
My resolution, love, shall be thy boast,
By whose example thou reveng'd mayst be.
How Tarquin must be us'd, read it in me:
   Myself, thy friend, will kill myself, thy foe,   1196
   And for my sake serve thou false Tarquin so.

'This brief abridgement of my will I make:
My soul and body to the skies and ground;
My resolution, husband, do thou take;   1200
Mine honour be the knife's that makes my wound;
My shame be his that did my fame confound;
   And all my fame that lives disbursed be
   To those that live, and think no shame of me.   1204

'Thou, Collatine, shalt oversee this will;
How was I overseen that thou shalt see it!
My blood shall wash the slander of mine ill;
My life's foul deed, my life's fair end shall free
   it.   1208
Faint not, faint heart, but stoutly say, "So be it":
   Yield to my hand; my hand shall conquer thee:
   Thou dead, both die, and both shall victors be.'

This plot of death when sadly she had laid,   1212
And wip'd the brinish pearl from her bright eyes,

1186 deprive: *take away*   1188-1190 *Cf. n.*
1196 thy foe; *cf. n.*   1199 *Cf. n.*   1205 oversee; *cf. n*
1206 overseen: *deceived*   1207 slander: *disgrace*

With untun'd tongue she hoarsely call'd her maid,
Whose swift obedience to her mistress hies;
For fleet-wing'd duty with thought's feathers flies. 1216
    Poor Lucrece' cheeks unto her maid seem so
    As winter meads when sun doth melt their snow.

Her mistress she doth give demure good-morrow,
With soft slow tongue, true mark of modesty,   1220
And sorts a sad look to her lady's sorrow,
For why her face wore sorrow's livery;
But durst not ask of her audaciously
    Why her two suns were cloud-eclipsed so,   1224
    Nor why her fair cheeks over-wash'd witb woe.

But as the earth doth weep, the sun being set,
Each flower moisten'd like a melting eye;
Even so the maid with swelling drops gan wet   1228
Her circled eyne, enforc'd by sympathy
Of those fair suns set in her mistress' sky,
    Who in a salt-wav'd ocean quench their light,
    Which makes the maid weep like the dewy
      night.   1232

A pretty while these pretty creatures stand,
Like ivory conduits coral cisterns filling;
One justly weeps, the other takes in hand
No cause but company of her drops spilling;   1236
Their gentle sex to weep are often willing,
    Grieving themselves to guess at others' smarts,
    And then they drown their eyes or break their
      hearts:

For men have marble, women waxen minds,   1240
And therefore are they form'd as marble will;

1219 demure: *modest*   1220 *Cf. n.*   1221 sorts: *adapts*
1222 For why: *because*   1234 *Cf. n.*   1235 justly: *with just cause*

The weak oppress'd, the impression of strange kinds
Is form'd in them by force, by fraud, or skill:
Then call them not the authors of their ill,   1244
   No more than wax shall be accounted evil
   Wherein is stamp'd the semblance of a devil.

Their smoothness, like a goodly champaign plain,
Lays open all the little worms that creep;   1248
In men, as in a rough-grown grove, remain
Cave-keeping evils that obscurely sleep:
Through crystal walls each little mote will peep:
   Though men can cover crimes with bold stern
            looks,   1252
   Poor women's faces are their own faults' books.

No man inveigh against the wither'd flower,
But chide rough winter that the flower hath kill'd:
Not that devour'd, but that which doth devour,   1256
Is worthy blame. O let it not be hild
Poor women's faults, that they are so fulfill'd
   With men's abuses: those proud lords, to blame,
   Make weak-made women tenants to their shame. 1260

The precedent whereof in Lucrece view,
Assail'd by night with circumstances strong
Of present death, and shame that might ensue
By that her death, to do her husband wrong: 1264
Such danger to resistance did belong,
   That dying fear through all her body spread;
   And who cannot abuse a body dead?

By this, mild patience bid fair Lucrece speak   1268
To the poor counterfeit of her complaining:

1247 champaign: *flat, open*   1257 hild: *i.e. held*
1261 *Cf. n.*   precedent: *proof*   1261-1267 *Cf. n.*
1269 counterfeit: *portrait*

'My girl,' quoth she, 'on what occasion break
Those tears from thee, that down thy cheeks are rain-
    ing?
If thou dost weep for grief of my sustaining,   1272
  Know, gentle wench, it small avails my mood:
  If tears could help, mine own would do me good.

'But tell me, girl, when went'—and there she stay'd
Till after a deep groan—'Tarquin from hence?'— 1276
'Madam, ere I was up,' replied the maid,
'The more to blame my sluggard negligence:
Yet with the fault I thus far can dispense;
  Myself was stirring ere the break of day,   1280
  And, ere I rose, was Tarquin gone away.

'But, lady, if your maid may be so bold,
She would request to know your heaviness.'
'O! peace,' quoth Lucrece; 'if it should be told, 1284
The repetition cannot make it less;
For more it is than I can well express:
  And that deep torture may be call'd a hell,
  When more is felt than one hath power to tell. 1288

'Go, get me hither paper, ink, and pen:
Yet save that labour, for I have them here.
What should I say? One of my husband's men
Bid thou be ready by and by, to bear   1292
A letter to my lord, my love, my dear:
  Bid him with speed prepare to carry it;
  The cause craves haste, and it will soon be writ.'

Her maid is gone, and she prepares to write,   1296
First hovering o'er the paper with her quill:
Conceit and grief an eager combat fight;

1272 of my sustaining: *which I sustain*
1279 dispense: *be excused*
                             1298 Conceit: *thought*

What wit sets down is blotted straight with will;
This is too curious-good, this blunt and ill: 1300
    Much like a press of people at a door,
    Throng her inventions, which shall go before.

At last she thus begins: 'Thou worthy lord
Of that unworthy wife that greeteth thee,   1304
Health to thy person! next vouchsafe t' afford,
If ever, love, thy Lucrece thou wilt see,
Some present speed to come and visit me.
    So I commend me from our house in grief: 1308
    My woes are tedious, though my words are brief.'

Here folds she up the tenour of her woe,
Her certain sorrow writ uncertainly.
By this short schedule Collatine may know   1312
Her grief, but not her grief's true quality:
She dares not thereof make discovery,
    Lest he should hold it her own gross abuse,
    Ere she with blood had stain'd her stain'd excuse.   1316

Besides, the life and feeling of her passion
She hoards, to spend when he is by to hear her;
When sighs, and groans, and tears may grace the fashion
Of her disgrace, the better so to clear her   1320
From that suspicion which the world might bear her.
    To shun this blot, she would not blot the letter
    With words, till action might become them better.

To see sad sights moves more than hear them told; 1324
For then the eye interprets to the ear
The heavy motion that it doth behold,

1300 curious-good: *well expressed but far-fetched*
1324 *Cf. n.*
                                  1326 motion: *action*

When every part a part of woe doth bear:
'Tis but a part of sorrow that we hear;   1328
   Deep sounds make lesser noise than shallow fords,
   And sorrow ebbs, being blown with wind of words.

Her letter now is seal'd, and on it writ
'At Ardea to my lord, with more than haste.'   1332
The post attends, and she delivers it,
Charging the sour-fac'd groom to hie as fast
As lagging fowls before the northern blast.
   Speed more than speed but dull and slow she
      deems: 1336
   Extremity still urgeth such extremes.

The homely villain curtsies to her low;
And, blushing on her, with a steadfast eye
Receives the scroll without or yea or no,   1340
And forth with bashful innocence doth hie:
But they whose guilt within their bosoms lie
   Imagine every eye beholds their blame;
   For Lucrece thought he blush'd to see her
      shame: 1344

When, silly groom! God wot, it was defect
Of spirit, life, and bold audacity.
Such harmless creatures have a true respect
To talk in deeds, while other saucily   1348
Promise more speed, but do it leisurely:
   Even so this pattern of the worn-out age
   Pawn'd honest looks, but laid no words to gage.

His kindled duty kindled her mistrust,   1352
That two red fires in both their faces blaz'd;

1333 attends: *waits*   1338 homely villain: *simple bondman*
1342 *Cf. n.*   1345 silly: *rustic*
1350 pattern: *exemplar*

She thought he blush'd, as knowing Tarquin's lust,
And, blushing with him, wistly on him gaz'd;
Her earnest eye did make him more amaz'd: 1356
  The more she saw the blood his cheeks replenish,
  The more she thought he spied in her some blemish.

But long she thinks till he return again,
And yet the duteous vassal scarce is gone.   1360
The weary time she cannot entertain,
For now 'tis stale to sigh, to weep, and groan:
So woe hath wearied woe, moan tired moan,
  That she her plaints a little while doth stay,   1364
  Pausing for means to mourn some newer way.

At last she calls to mind where hangs a piece
Of skilful painting, made for Priam's Troy;
Before the which is drawn the power of Greece,   1368
For Helen's rape the city to destroy,
Threat'ning cloud-kissing Ilion with annoy;
  Which the conceited painter drew so proud,
  As heaven, it seem'd, to kiss the turrets bow'd. 1372

A thousand lamentable objects there,
In scorn of nature, art gave lifeless life;
Many a dry drop seem'd a weeping tear,
Shed for the slaughter'd husband by the wife: 1376
The red blood reek'd, to show the painter's strife;
  And dying eyes gleam'd forth their ashy lights,
  Like dying coals burnt out in tedious nights.

There might you see the labouring pioner,   1380
Begrim'd with sweat, and smeared all with dust;
And from the towers of Troy there would appear

1355 wistly: *intently*   1366 ff. *Cf. n.*   1367 painting; *cf. n.*
1370 annoy: *injury*   1371 conceited: *imaginative*
1377 strife: *emulation*   1380 pioner: *sapper*

The very eyes of men through loop-holes thrust,
Gazing upon the Greeks with little lust: 1384
    Such sweet observance in this work was had,
    That one might see those far-off eyes look sad.

In great commanders grace and majesty
You might behold, triumphing in their faces;   1388
In youth quick bearing and dexterity;
And here and there the painter interlaces
Pale cowards, marching on with trembling paces;
    Which heartless peasants did so well resemble, 1392
    That one would swear he saw them quake and tremble.

In Ajax and Ulysses, O, what art
Of physiognomy might one behold!
The face of either cipher'd either's heart;   1396
Their face their manners most expressly told:
    In Ajax' eyes blunt rage and rigour roll'd;
    But the mild glance that sly Ulysses lent
    Show'd deep regard and smiling government.   1400

There pleading might you see grave Nestor stand,
As 'twere encouraging the Greeks to fight;
Making such sober action with his hand,
That it beguil'd attention, charm'd the sight.   1404
In speech, it seem'd, his beard, all silver white,
    Wagg'd up and down, and from his lips did fly
    Thin winding breath, which purl'd up to the sky.

About him were a press of gaping faces,   1408
Which seem'd to swallow up his sound advice;
All jointly listening, but with several graces,

1384 lust: *pleasure*   1385 observance: *observant care*
1396 cipher'd: *expressed*
1400 regard: *reflection*   government: *self-command*
1403 action: *gesture*
                                            1407 purl'd: *curled*

As if some mermaid did their ears entice,
Some high, some low, the painter was so nice;   1412
    The scalps of many, almost hid behind,
    To jump up higher seem'd, to mock the mind.

Here one man's hand lean'd on another's head,
His nose being shadow'd by his neighbour's ear;   1416
Here one being throng'd bears back, all boll'n and red;
Another smother'd, seems to pelt and swear;
And in their rage such signs of rage they bear,
    As, but for loss of Nestor's golden words,   1420
    It seem'd they would debate with angry swords.

For much imaginary work was there;
Conceit deceitful, so compact, so kind,
That for Achilles' image stood his spear,   1424
Grip'd in an armed hand; himself behind,
Was left unseen, save to the eye of mind:
    A hand, a foot, a face, a leg, a head,
    Stood for the whole to be imagined.   1428

And from the walls of strong-besieged Troy,
When their brave hope, bold Hector, march'd to field,
Stood many Troyan mothers, sharing joy
To see their youthful sons bright weapons wield;   1432
And to their hope they such odd action yield,
    That through their light joy seemed to appear,—
    Like bright things stain'd—a kind of heavy fear.

And, from the strand of Dardan, where they fought,   1436
To Simois' reedy banks the red blood ran,

1414 mock: *work illusion in*
1417 throng'd: *pressed*   boll'n: *swollen*
1418 pelt: *throw out angry words*   1421 debate: *fight*
1423 compact: *well composed*   kind: *natural*
1435 stain'd: *tarnished*   1436 Dardan; *cf. n.*
1437 Simois; *cf. n.*

Whose waves to imitate the battle sought
With swelling ridges; and their ranks began
To break upon the galled shore, and than   1440
   Retire again, till meeting greater ranks
   They join and shoot their foam at Simois' banks.

To this well-painted piece is Lucrece come,
To find a face where all distress is stell'd.   1444
Many she sees where cares have carved some,
But none where all distress and dolour dwell'd,
Till she despairing Hecuba beheld,
   Staring on Priam's wounds with her old eyes,   1448
   Which bleeding under Pyrrhus' proud foot lies.

In her the painter had anatomiz'd
Time's ruin, beauty's wrack, and grim care's reign:
Her cheeks with chaps and wrinkles were dis-
      guis'd;   1452
Of what she was no semblance did remain;
Her blue blood chang'd to black in every vein,
   Wanting the spring that those shrunk pipes had fed,
   Show'd life imprison'd in a body dead.   1456

On this sad shadow Lucrece spends her eyes,
And shapes her sorrow to the beldam's woes,
Who nothing wants to answer her but cries,
And bitter words to ban her cruel foes: 1460
The painter was no god to lend her those;
   And therefore Lucrece swears he did her wrong,
   To give her so much grief and not a tongue.

'Poor instrument,' quoth she, 'without a sound,   1464
I'll tune thy woes with my lamenting tongue,

1440 galled: *fretted*   than: *then*   1444 stell'd: *delineated*
1450 anatomiz'd: *represented minutely*   1450, 1451 *Cf. n.*
1457 shadow: *image*

And drop sweet balm in Priam's painted wound,
And rail on Pyrrhus that hath done him wrong,
And with my tears quench Troy that burns so
    long,   1468
    And with my knife scratch out the angry eyes
    Of all the Greeks that are thine enemies.

'Show me the strumpet that began this stir,
That with my nails her beauty I may tear.   1472
Thy heat of lust, fond Paris, did incur
This load of wrath that burning Troy doth bear:
Thy eye kindled the fire that burneth here;
    And here in Troy, for trespass of thine eye,   1476
    The sire, the son, the dame, and daughter die.

'Why should the private pleasure of some one
Become the public plague of many moe?
Let sin, alone committed, light alone   1480
Upon his head that hath transgressed so;
Let guiltless souls be freed from guilty woe;
    For one's offence why should so many fall,
    To plague a private sin in general?   1484

'Lo! here weeps Hecuba, here Priam dies,
Here manly Hector faints, here Troilus swounds,
Here friend by friend in bloody channel lies,
And friend to friend gives unadvised wounds,   1488
And one man's lust these many lives confounds:
    Had doting Priam check'd his son's desire,
    Troy had been bright with fame and not with fire.'

Here feelingly she weeps Troy's painted woes; 1492
For sorrow, like a heavy-hanging bell,
Once set on ringing, with his own weight goes;

1479 moe: *more*   1486 swounds: *swoons*
1488 unadvised: *unintentional*

Then little strength rings out the doleful knell:
So Lucrece, set a-work, sad tales doth tell   1496
  To pencil'd pensiveness and colour'd sorrow;
  She lends them words, and she their looks doth bor-
    row.

She throws her eyes about the painting round,
And whom she finds forlorn she doth lament: 1500
At last she sees a wretched image bound,
That piteous looks to Phrygian shepherds lent;
His face, though full of cares, yet show'd content;
  Onward to Troy with the blunt swains he goes, 1504
  So mild, that Patience seem'd to scorn his woes.

In him the painter labour'd with his skill
To hide deceit, and give the harmless show
An humble gait, calm looks, eyes wailing still,   1508
A brow unbent that seem'd to welcome woe;
Cheeks neither red nor pale, but mingled so
  That blushing red no guilty instance gave,
  Nor ashy pale the fear that false hearts have.   1512

But, like a constant and confirmed devil,
He entertain'd a show so seeming-just,
And therein so ensconc'd his secret evil,
That jealousy itself could not mistrust   1516
False-creeping craft and perjury should thrust
  Into so bright a day such black-fac'd storms,
  Or blot with hell-born sin such saint-like forms.

The well-skill'd workman this mild image drew   1520
For perjur'd Sinon, whose enchanting story
The credulous old Priam after slew;

1497 pencil'd: *painted*   1501 wretched image; *cf. n.*
1514 entertain'd: *kept up*   1516 jealousy: *suspicion*

Whose words, like wildfire, burnt the shining glory
Of rich-built Ilion, that the skies were sorry,   1524
    And little stars shot from their fixed places,
    When their glass fell wherein they view'd their
        faces.

This picture she advisedly perus'd,
And chid the painter for his wondrous skill,   1528
Saying, some shape in Sinon's was abus'd;
So fair a form lodg'd not a mind so ill:
And still on him she gaz'd, and gazing still,
    Such signs of truth in his plain face she spied, 1532
    That she concludes the picture was belied.

'It cannot be,' quoth she, 'that so much guile,'—
She would have said,—'can lurk in such a look';
But Tarquin's shape came in her mind the while, 1536
And from her tongue 'can lurk' from 'cannot' took:
'It cannot be,' she in that sense forsook,
    And turn'd it thus, 'It cannot be, I find,
    But such a face should bear a wicked mind: 1540

'For even as subtle Sinon here is painted,
So sober-sad, so weary, and so mild,
As if with grief or travail he had fainted,
To me came Tarquin armed to beguild   1544
With outward honesty, but yet defil'd
    With inward vice: as Priam him did cherish,
    So did I Tarquin; so my Troy did perish.

'Look, look, how listening Priam wets his eyes,   1548
To see those borrow'd tears that Sinon sheds!
Priam, why art thou old and yet not wise?

1523 wildfire; *cf. n.*   1525 *Cf. n.*
1526 their glass; *cf. n.*   1527 advisedly: *intently*
1544 to beguild; *cf. n.*

For every tear he falls a Troyan bleeds:
His eye drops fire, no water thence proceeds; 1552
  Those round clear pearls of his, that move thy pity,
  Are balls of quenchless fire to burn thy city.

'Such devils steal effects from lightless hell;
For Sinon in his fire doth quake with cold, 1556
And in that cold hot-burning fire doth dwell;
These contraries such unity do hold,
Only to flatter fools and make them bold:
  So Priam's trust false Sinon's tears doth flatter, 1560
  That he finds means to burn his Troy with water.'

Here, all enrag'd, such passion her assails,
That patience is quite beaten from her breast.
She tears the senseless Sinon with her nails, 1564
Comparing him to that unhappy guest
Whose deed hath made herself herself detest:
  At last she smilingly with this gives o'er;
  'Fool, fool!' quoth she, 'his wounds will not be
    sore.' 1568

Thus ebbs and flows the current of her sorrow,
And time doth weary time with her complaining.
She looks for night, and then she longs for morrow,
And both she thinks too long with her remaining: 1572
Short time seems long in sorrow's sharp sustaining:
  Though woe be heavy, yet it seldom sleeps;
  And they that watch see time how slow it creeps.

Which all this time hath overslipp'd her thought, 1576
That she with painted images hath spent;
Being from the feeling of her own grief brought
By deep surmise of others' detriment;

1551 falls: *sheds*

Losing her woes in shows of discontent.					1580
   It easeth some, though none it ever cur'd,
   To think their dolour others have endur'd.

But now the mindful messenger, come back,
Brings home his lord and other company;					1584
Who finds his Lucrece clad in mourning black;
And round about her tear-distained eye
Blue circles stream'd, like rainbows in the sky:
   These water-galls in her dim element					1588
   Foretell new storms to those already spent.

Which when her sad-beholding husband saw,
Amazedly in her sad face he stares:
Her eyes, though sod in tears, look'd red and raw, 1592
Her lively colour kill'd with deadly cares.
He hath no power to ask her how she fares:
   Both stood like old acquaintance in a trance,
   Met far from home, wondering each other's
      chance.					1596

At last he takes her by the bloodless hand,
And thus begins: 'What uncouth ill event
Hath thee befall'n, that thou dost trembling stand?
Sweet love, what spite hath thy fair colour spent? 1600
Why art thou thus attir'd in discontent?
   Unmask, dear dear, this moody heaviness,
   And tell thy grief, that we may give redress.'

Three times with sighs she gives her sorrow fire,	1604
Ere once she can discharge one word of woe:
At length address'd to answer his desire,

1585 mourning; *cf. n.*					1588 water-galls; *cf. n.*
1593 lively: *living*					1598 uncouth: *unknown*
1600 spite: *trouble*					1602 moody: *gloomy*
1604 *Cf. n.*					1606 address'd: *ready*

She modestly prepares to let them know
Her honour is ta'en prisoner by the foe;   1608
   While Collatine and his consorted lords
   With sad attention long to hear her words.

And now this pale swan in her watery nest
Begins the sad dirge of her certain ending.   1612
'Few words,' quoth she, 'shall fit the trespass best,
Where no excuse can give the fault amending:
In me moe woes than words are now depending;
   And my laments would be drawn out too long,   1616
   To tell them all with one poor tired tongue.

'Then be this all the task it hath to say:
Dear husband, in the interest of thy bed
A stranger came, and on that pillow lay   1620
Where thou wast wont to rest thy weary head;
And what wrong else may be imagined
   By foul enforcement might be done to me,
   From that, alas! thy Lucrece is not free.   1624

'For in the dreadful dead of dark midnight,
With shining falchion in my chamber came
A creeping creature with a flaming light,
And softly cried, "Awake, thou Roman dame,   1628
And entertain my love; else lasting shame
   On thee and thine this night I will inflict,
   If thou my love's desire do contradict.

' "For some hard-favour'd groom of thine," quoth
   he,   1632
"Unless thou yoke thy liking to my will,
I'll murther straight, and then I'll slaughter thee,
And swear I found you where you did fulfil

1615 depending: *imminent*
1619 interest: *possession*

1620 *Cf. n.*

The loathsome act of lust, and so did kill   1636
　　The lechers in their deed: this act will be
　　My fame, and thy perpetual infamy."

'With this I did begin to start and cry,
And then against my heart he set his sword,   1640
Swearing, unless I took all patiently,
I should not live to speak another word;
So should my shame still rest upon record,
　　And never be forgot in mighty Rome   1644
　　The adulterate death of Lucrece and her groom.

'Mine enemy was strong, my poor self weak,
And far the weaker with so strong a fear:
My bloody judge forbade my tongue to speak;   1648
No rightful plea might plead for justice there:
His scarlet lust came evidence to swear
　　That my poor beauty had purloin'd his eyes;
　　And when the judge is robb'd the prisoner dies. 1652

'O, teach me how to make mine own excuse,
Or, at the least, this refuge let me find:
Though my gross blood be stain'd with this abuse,
Immaculate and spotless is my mind;   1656
That was not forc'd; that never was inclin'd
　　To accessary yieldings, but still pure
　　Doth in her poison'd closet yet endure.'

Lo! here the helpless merchant of this loss,   1660
With head declin'd, and voice damm'd up with woe,
With sad-set eyes, and wretched arms across,
From lips new-waxen pale begins to blow
The grief away that stops his answer so: 1664
　　But, wretched as he is, he strives in vain;
　　What he breathes out his breath drinks up again.

1645 adulterate: *adulterous*　　　　　　　　1650 scarlet; *cf. n.*
1655, 1656 *Cf. n.*　　　　　　　　　　　　　1660 ff. *Cf. n.*

As through an arch the violent roaring tide
Outruns the eye that doth behold his haste,　　1668
Yet in the eddy boundeth in his pride
Back to the strait that forc'd him on so fast;
In rage sent out, recall'd in rage, being past:
　　Even so his sighs, his sorrows, make a saw,　　1672
　　To push grief on, and back the same grief draw.

Which speechless woe of his poor she attendeth,
And his untimely frenzy thus awaketh:
'Dear lord, thy sorrow to my sorrow lendeth　　1676
Another power; no flood by raining slaketh.
My woe too sensible thy passion maketh
　　More feeling-painful: let it then suffice,
　　To drown one woe, one pair of weeping eyes. 1680

'And for my sake, when I might charm thee so,
For she that was thy Lucrece, now attend me:
Be suddenly revenged on my foe,
Thine, mine, his own: suppose thou dost defend me 1684
From what is past: the help that thou shalt lend me
　　Comes all too late, yet let the traitor die;
　　For sparing justice feeds iniquity.

'But ere I name him, you, fair lords,' quoth she,— 1688
Speaking to those that came with Collatine,—
'Shall plight your honourable faiths to me,
With swift pursuit to venge this wrong of mine;
For 'tis a meritorious fair design　　　　1692
　　To chase injustice with revengeful arms:
　　Knights, by their oaths, should right poor ladies'
　　　　harms.

At this request, with noble disposition
Each present lord began to promise aid,　　1696

1672, 1673 *Cf. n.*　　　　　　1689-1691 *Cf. n.*

As bound in knighthood to her imposition,
Longing to hear the hateful foe bewray'd:
But she, that yet her sad task hath not said,
  The protestation stops. 'O, speak!' quoth she,   1700
  'How may this forced stain be wip'd from me?

'What is the quality of mine offence,
Being constrain'd with dreadful circumstance?
May my pure mind with the foul act dispense,   1704
My low-declined honour to advance?
May any terms acquit me from this chance?
  The poison'd fountain clears itself again;
  And why not I from this compelled stain?'   1708

With this, they all at once began to say,
Her body's stain her mind untainted clears;
While with a joyless smile she turns away
The face, that map which deep impression bears   1712
Of hard misfortune, carv'd in it with tears.
  'No, no,' quoth she, 'no dame, hereafter living,
  By my excuse shall claim excuse's giving.'

Here with a sigh, as if her heart would break,   1716
She throws forth Tarquin's name. 'He, he,' she says,
But more than 'he' her poor tongue could not speak;
Till after many accents and delays,
Untimely breathings, sick and short assays,   1720
  She utters this, 'He, he, fair lords, 'tis he,
  That guides this hand to give this wound to me.'

Even here she sheathed in her harmless breast
A harmful knife, that thence her soul unsheath'd: 1724
That blow did bail it from the deep unrest

1697 imposition: *command*   1706 chance: *mischance*
1709, 1710 Cf. n.
1720 Untimely: *irregular*   1714, 1715 Cf. n.

Of that polluted prison where it breath'd;
Her contrite sighs unto the clouds bequeath'd
> Her winged sprite, and through her wounds doth
> fly   1728
> Life's lasting date from cancell'd destiny.

Stone-still, astonish'd with this deadly deed,
Stood Collatine and all his lordly crew;
Till Lucrece' father, that beholds her bleed,   1732
Himself on her self-slaughter'd body threw;
And from the purple fountain Brutus drew
> The murderous knife, and as it left the place,
> Her blood, in poor revenge, held it in chase;   1736

And bubbling from her breast, it doth divide
In two slow rivers, that the crimson blood
Circles her body in on every side,
Who, like a late-sack'd island, vastly stood,   1740
Bare and unpeopled in this fearful flood.
> Some of her blood still pure and red remain'd,
> And some look'd black, and that false Tarquin
> stain'd.

About the mourning and congealed face,   1744
Of that black blood a watery rigol goes,
Which seems to weep upon the tainted place:
And ever since, as pitying Lucrece' woes,
Corrupted blood some watery token shows;   1748
> And blood untainted still doth red abide,
> Blushing at that which is so putrefied.

'Daughter, dear daughter!' old Lucretius cries,
'That life was mine which thou hast here depriv'd. 1752
If in the child the father's image lies,

Where shall I live now Lucrece is unliv'd?
Thou wast not to this end from me deriv'd.
   If children predecease progenitors,   **1756**
   We are their offspring, and they none of ours.

'Poor broken glass, I often did behold
In thy sweet semblance my old age new born;
But now that fair fresh mirror, dim and old,   **1760**
Shows me a bare-bon'd death by time outworn.
O! from thy cheeks my image thou hast torn,
   And shiver'd all the beauty of my glass,
   That I no more can see what once I was.   **1764**

'O Time! cease thou thy course, and last no longer,
If they surcease to be that should survive.
Shall rotten death make conquest of the stronger,
And leave the faltering feeble souls alive?   **1768**
The old bees die, the young possess their hive:
   Then live, sweet Lucrece, live again and see
   Thy father die, and not thy father thee!'

By this, starts Collatine as from a dream,   **1772**
And bids Lucretius give his sorrow place;
And then in key-cold Lucrece' bleeding stream
He falls, and bathes the pale fear in his face,
And counterfeits to die with her a space;   **1776**
   Till manly shame bids him possess his breath
   And live to be revenged on her death.

The deep vexation of his inward soul
Hath serv'd a dumb arrest upon his tongue;   **1780**
Who, mad that sorrow should his use control
Or keep him from heart-easing words so long,

1759 semblance: *likeness*   1761 death: *representation of Death*
1766 surcease: *cease*   1772-1775 *Cf. n.*

Begins to talk; but through his lips do throng
    Weak words so thick, come in his poor heart's
        aid,   1784
    That no man could distinguish what he said.

Yet sometime 'Tarquin' was pronounced plain,
But through his teeth, as if the name he tore.
This windy tempest, till it blow up rain,   1788
Held back his sorrow's tide to make it more;
At last it rains, and busy winds give o'er:
    Then son and father weep with equal strife
    Who should weep most, for daughter or for
        wife.   1792

The one doth call her his, the other his,
Yet neither may possess the claim they lay.
The father says, 'She's mine.' 'O! mine she is,'
Replies her husband; 'do not take away   1796
My sorrow's interest; let no mourner say
    He weeps for her, for she was only mine,
    And only must be wail'd by Collatine.'

'O!' quoth Lucretius, 'I did give that life   1800
Which she too early and too late hath spill'd.'
'Woe, woe,' quoth Collatine, 'she was my wife,
I ow'd her, and 'tis mine that she hath kill'd.'
'My daughter' and 'my wife' with clamours fill'd 1804
    The dispers'd air, who, holding Lucrece' life,
    Answer'd their cries, 'my daughter' and 'my wife.

Brutus, who pluck'd the knife from Lucrece' side,
Seeing such emulation in their woe,   1808
Began to clothe his wit in state and pride,
Burying in Lucrece' wound his folly's show.

1797 interest; *cf. n.*   1801 late: *recently*   spill'd: *destroyed*
1803 ow'd: *owned*   1809, 1810 *Cf. n.*

He with the Romans was esteemed so
   As silly-jeering idiots are with kings,   1812
  For sportive words and uttering foolish things:

But now he throws that shallow habit by,
Wherein deep policy did him disguise;
And arm'd his long-hid wits advisedly,   1816
To check the tears in Collatinus' eyes.
'Thou wronged lord of Rome,' quoth he, 'arise:
   Let my unsounded self, suppos'd a fool,
   Now set thy long-experienc'd wit to school.   1820

'Why, Collatine, is woe the cure for woe?
Do wounds help wounds, or grief help grievous deeds?
Is it revenge to give thyself a blow
For his foul act by whom thy fair wife bleeds?   1824
Such childish humour from weak minds proceeds:
   Thy wretched wife mistook the matter so,
   To slay herself, that should have slain her foe.

'Courageous Roman, do not steep thy heart   1828
In such relenting dew of lamentations;
But kneel with me and help to bear thy part,
To rouse our Roman gods with invocations,
That they will suffer these abominations,   1832
   Since Rome herself in them doth stand disgrac'd,
   By our strong arms from forth her fair streets
     chas'd.

'Now, by the Capitol that we adore,
And by this chaste blood so unjustly stain'd,   1836
By heaven's fair sun that breeds the fat earth's store,
By all our country rights in Rome maintain'd,
And by chaste Lucrece' soul, that late complain'd
   Her wrongs to us, and by this bloody knife,   1840
   We will revenge the death of this true wife.'

This said, he struck his hand upon his breast,
And kiss'd the fatal knife to end his vow;
And to his protestation urg'd the rest,   1844
Who, wondering at him, did his words allow:
Then jointly to the ground their knees they bow;
  And that deep vow, which Brutus made before,
  He doth again repeat, and that they swore.   1848

When they had sworn to this advised doom,
They did conclude to bear dead Lucrece thence;
To show her bleeding body thorough Rome,
And so to publish Tarquin's foul offence: 1852
Which being done with speedy diligence,
  The Romans plausibly did give consent
  To Tarquin's everlasting banishment.

1843-1848 *Cf. n.*   1845 allow: *approve*
1850, 1851 *Cf. n.*   1854 plausibly: *approvingly*

FINIS.

The Phœnix and the Turtle

LET the bird of loudest lay,
On the sole Arabian tree,
Herald sad and trumpet be,
To whose sound chaste wings obey.   **4**

But thou shrieking harbinger,
Foul precurrer of the fiend,
Augur of the fever's end,
To this troop come thou not near.   **8**

From this session interdict
Every fowl of tyrant wing,
Save the eagle, feather'd king:
Keep the obsequy so strict.   **12**

Let the priest in surplice white,
That defunctive music can,
Be the death-divining swan,
Lest the requiem lack his right.   **16**

And thou treble-dated crow,
That thy sable gender mak'st
With the breath thou giv'st and tak'st,
'Mongst our mourners shalt thou go.   **20**

Here the anthem doth commence:
Love and constancy is dead;
Phœnix and the turtle fled
In a mutual flame from hence.   **24**

---

1 bird of loudest lay; *cf. n.*   2 Arabian tree; *cf. n.*
3 trumpet: *trumpeter*   5 shrieking harbinger; *cf. n.*
6 precurrer: *forerunner*   9 interdict: *forbid*
10 tyrant wing; *cf. n.*   14 defunctive: *funereal*   can: *knows*
15 death-divining; *cf. n.*   17 treble-dated; *cf. n.*
18 sable: *black; cf. n.*

So they lov'd, as love in twain
Had the essence but in one;
Two distincts, division none:
Number there in love was slain.   28

Hearts remote, yet not asunder;
Distance, and no space was seen
'Twixt the turtle and his queen:
But in them it were a wonder.   32

So between them love did shine,
That the turtle saw his right
Flaming in the phœnix' sight;
Either was the other's mine.   36

Property was thus appall'd,
That the self was not the same;
Single nature's double name
Neither two nor one was call'd.   40

Reason, in itself confounded,
Saw division grow together;
To themselves yet either neither,
Simple were so well compounded,   44

That it cried, 'How true a twain
Seemeth this concordant one!
Love hath reason, reason none,
If what parts can so remain.'   48

Whereupon it made this threne
To the phœnix and the dove,
Co-supremes and stars of love,
As chorus to their tragic scene.   52

25-28 *Cf. n.*   29, 30 *Cf. n.*
32 But: *except*   were: *would be; cf. n.*   33-36 *Cf. n.*
37-40 *Cf. n.*   41 confounded: *defeated*
42 *Cf. n.*   44 compounded: *blended*
43-46 *Cf. n.*   47, 48 *Cf. n.*   49 threne: *dirge*

THRENOS.

Beauty, truth, and rarity,
Grace in all simplicity,
Here enclos'd in cinders lie.

Death is now the phœnix' nest;   56
And the turtle's loyal breast
To eternity doth rest,

Leaving no posterity:
'Twas not their infirmity,   60
It was married chastity.

Truth may seem, but cannot be;
Beauty brag, but 'tis not she;
Truth and beauty buried be.   64

To this urn let those repair
That are either true or fair;
For these dead birds, sigh a prayer.

Threnos: *dirge*
53 rarity: *uncommon excellence*

The Passionate Pilgrim

I.

WHEN my love swears that she is made of truth,
I do believe her, though I know she lies,
That she might think me some untutor'd youth,
Unskilful in the world's false forgeries.   4
Thus vainly thinking that she thinks me young,
Although I know my years be past the best,
I smiling credit her false-speaking tongue,
Outfacing faults in love with love's ill rest.   8
But wherefore says my love that she is young?
And wherefore say not I that I am old?
O! love's best habit is a soothing tongue,
And age, in love, loves not to have years told.   12
    Therefore I'll lie with love, and love with me,
    Since that our faults in love thus smother'd be.

II.

Two loves I have of comfort and despair,
Which like two spirits do suggest me still;
The better angel is a man, right fair,
The worser spirit a woman, colour'd ill.   4
To win me soon to hell, my female evil
Tempteth my better angel from my side,
And would corrupt a saint to be a devil,
Wooing his purity with her fair pride: 8
And whether that my angel be turn'd fiend
Suspect I may, but not directly tell;
For being both to me, both to each friend,

I. *Cf. n.*
II. *Cf. n.*   2 suggest: *tempt*   8 ill rest: *poor remnant*
    11 *Cf. n.*

I guess one angel in another's hell.   12
   The truth I shall not know, but live in doubt,
   Till my bad angel fire my good one out.

III.

Did not the heavenly rhetoric of thine eye,
'Gainst whom the world could not hold argument,
Persuade my heart to this false perjury?
Vows for thee broke deserve not punishment.   4
A woman I forswore; but I will prove,
Thou being a goddess, I forswore not thee:
My vow was earthly, thou a heavenly love;
Thy grace being gain'd cures all disgrace in me.   8
My vow was breath, and breath a vapour is;
Then thou, fair sun, that on this earth dost shine,
Exhale this vapour vow; in thee it is:
If broken, then it is no fault of mine.   12
   If by me broke, what fool is not so wise
   To break an oath, to win a paradise?

IV.

Sweet Cytherea, sitting by a brook
With young Adonis, lovely, fresh, and green,
Did court the lad with many a lovely look,
Such looks as none could look but beauty's queen.   4
She told him stories to delight his ear;
She show'd him favours to allure his eye;
To win his heart, she touch'd him here and there,—
Touches so soft still conquer chastity.   8
But whether unripe years did want conceit,
Or he refus'd to take her figur'd proffer,
The tender nibbler would not touch the bait,

III. *Cf. n.*   IV. *Cf. n.*
9 conceit: *understanding*   10 figur'd: *made by signs*

But smile and jest at every gentle offer: 12
   Then fell she on her back, fair queen, and toward:
   He rose and ran away; ah! fool too froward.

V.

If love make he forsworn, how shall I swear to love?
O, never faith could hold, if not to beauty vow'd!
Though to myself forsworn, to thee I'll constant prove;
Those thoughts, to me like oaks, to thee like osiers
     bow'd.   4
Study his bias leaves, and makes his book thine eyes,
Where all those pleasures live that art can compre-
     hend.
If knowledge be the mark, to know thee shall suffice;
Well learned is that tongue that well can thee com-
     mend;   8
All ignorant that soul that sees thee without wonder;
Which is to me some praise, that I thy parts admire:
Thine eye Jove's lightning seems, thy voice his dread-
     ful thunder,
Which, not to anger bent, is music and sweet fire.   12
   Celestial as thou art, O! do not love that wrong,
   To sing heaven's praise with such an earthly tongue.

VI.

Scarce had the sun dried up the dewy morn,
And scarce the herd gone to the hedge for shade,
When Cytherea, all in love forlorn,
A longing tarriance for Adonis made   4
Under an osier growing by a brook,
A brook where Adon us'd to cool his spleen:
Hot was the day; she hotter that did look

V. *Cf. n.*   5 bias: *natural disposition*
VI. *Cf. n.*

For his approach, that often there had been.   8
Anon he comes, and throws his mantle by,
And stood stark naked on the brook's green brim:
The sun look'd on the world with glorious eye,
Yet not so wistly as this queen on him: 12
    He, spying her, bounc'd in, whereas he stood:
    'O Jove,' quoth she, 'why was not I a flood!'

VII.

Fair is my love, but not so fair as fickle;
Mild as a dove, but neither true nor trusty;
Brighter than glass, and yet, as glass is, brittle;
Softer than wax, and yet, as iron, rusty: 4
    A lily pale, with damask dye to grace her,
    None fairer, nor none falser to deface her.

Her lips to mine how often hath she join'd,
Between each kiss her oaths of true love swearing! 8
How many tales to please me hath she coin'd,
Dreading my love, the loss thereof still fearing!
    Yet in the midst of all her pure protestings,
    Her faith, her oaths, her tears, and all were jest-
      ings.   12

She burn'd with love, as straw with fire flameth;
She burn'd out love, as soon as straw outburneth;
She fram'd the love, and yet she foil'd the framing;
She bade love last, and yet she fell a-turning.   16
    Was this a lover, or a lecher whether?
    Bad in the best, though excellent in neither.

VIII.

If music and sweet poetry agree,
As they must needs, the sister and the brother,

12 wistly: *eagerly*   VII. *Cf. n.*   5 damask; *cf. n.*
VIII. *Cf. n.*

Then must the love be great 'twixt thee and me,
Because thou lov'st the one, and I the other. 4
Dowland to thee is dear, whose heavenly touch
Upon the lute doth ravish human sense;
Spenser to me, whose deep conceit is such
As, passing all conceit, needs no defence. 8
Thou lov'st to hear the sweet melodious sound
That Phœbus' lute, the queen of music, makes;
And I in deep delight am chiefly drown'd
Whenas himself to singing he betakes. 12
 One god is god of both, as poets feign;
 One knight loves both, and both in thee remain.

IX.

Fair was the morn when the fair queen of love,
 *   *   *   *   *   *   *
Paler for sorrow than her milk-white dove,
For Adon's sake, a youngster proud and wild; 4
Her stand she takes upon a steep-up hill:
Anon Adonis comes with horn and hounds;
She, silly queen, with more than love's good will,
Forbade the boy he should not pass those grounds: 8
'Once,' quoth she, 'did I see a fair sweet youth
Here in these brakes deep-wounded with a boar,
Deep in the thigh, a spectacle of ruth!
See, in my thigh,' quoth she, 'here was the sore.' 12
 She showed hers; he saw more wounds than one,
 And blushing fled, and left her all alone.

X.

Sweet rose, fair flower, untimely pluck'd, soon vaded,
Pluck'd in the bud, and vaded in the spring!

3 thee; *cf. n.*   5 Dowland; *cf. n.*   14 One knight; *cf. n.*
IX. *Cf. n.*   X. *Cf. n.*   1 vaded: *faded*

Bright orient pearl, alack! too timely shaded;
Fair creature, kill'd too soon by death's sharp sting! 4
   Like a green plum that hangs upon a tree,
   And falls, through wind, before the fall should be.

I weep for thee, and yet no cause I have;
For why thou left'st me nothing in thy will: 8
And yet thou left'st me more than I did crave;
For why I craved nothing of thee still:
   O yes, dear friend, I pardon crave of thee,
   Thy discontent thou didst bequeath to me. 12

XI.

Venus, with young Adonis sitting by her
Under a myrtle shade, began to woo him:
She told the youngling how god Mars did try her,
And as he fell to her, so fell she to him. 4
'Even thus,' quoth she, 'the warlike god embrac'd me,'
And then she clipp'd Adonis in her arms;
'Even thus,' quoth she, 'the warlike god unlac'd me,'
As if the boy should use like loving charms. 8
'Even thus,' quoth she, 'he seized on my lips,'
And with her lips on his did act the seizure;
And as she fetched breath, away he skips,
And would not take her meaning nor her pleasure. 12
   Ah! that I had my lady at this bay,
   To kiss and clip me till I run away.

XII.

Crabbed age and youth cannot live together:
Youth is full of pleasure, age is full of care;
Youth like summer morn, age like winter weather;
Youth like summer brave, age like winter bare. 4

XI. *Cf. n.*   6 clipp'd: *embraced*   9-12 *Cf. n.*
13 bay; *cf. n.*   XII. *Cf. n.*   4 brave: *adorned*

Youth is full of sport, age's breath is short;
  Youth is nimble, age is lame;
Youth is hot and bold, age is weak and cold;
Youth is wild, and age is tame.   8
Age, I do abhor thee, youth, I do adore thee;
  O, my love, my love is young!
Age, I do defy thee: O, sweet shepherd, hie thee,
  For methinks thou stay'st too long!   12

XIII.

Beauty is but a vain and doubtful good;
A shining gloss that vadeth suddenly;
A flower that dies when first it 'gins to bud;
A brittle glass that's broken presently: 4
  A doubtful good, a gloss, a glass, a flower,
  Lost, vaded, broken, dead within an hour.

And as goods lost are seld or never found,
As vaded gloss no rubbing will refresh,   8
As flowers dead lie wither'd on the ground,
As broken glass no cement can redress,
  So beauty blemish'd once 's for ever lost,
  In spite of physic, painting, pain, and cost.   12

XIV.

Good night, good rest. Ah! neither be my share:
She bade good night that kept my rest away;
And daff'd me to a cabin hang'd with care,
To descant on the doubts of my decay.   4
  'Farewell,' quoth she, 'and come again to-morrow:'
  Fare well I could not, for I supp'd with sorrow.

XIII. *Cf. n.*   2 vadeth; *cf.* X. 1   7 seld: *seldom*
XIV. *Cf. n.*   3 daff'd: *sent off*   4 descant: *comment*

Yet at my parting sweetly did she smile,
In scorn or friendship, nill I conster whether: 8
'T may be, she joy'd to jest at my exile,
'T may be, again to make me wander thither:
   'Wander,' a word for shadows like myself,
   As take the pain, but cannot pluck the pelf.   12

Lord! how mine eyes throw gazes to the east;
My heart doth charge the watch; the morning rise
Doth cite each moving sense from idle rest.
Not daring trust the office of mine eyes,   16
   While Philomela sits and sings, I sit and mark,
   And wish her lays were tuned like the lark;

For she doth welcome daylight with her ditty,
And drives away dark dismal-dreaming night: 20
The night so pack'd, I post unto my pretty;
Heart hath his hope, and eyes their wished sight;
   Sorrow chang'd to solace, solace mix'd with sorrow;
   For why, she sigh'd and bade me come to-morrow. 24

Were I with her, the night would post too soon;
But now are minutes added to the hours;
To spite me now, each minute seems a moon;
Yet not for me, shine sun to succour flowers!   28
   Pack night, peep day; good day, of night now bor-
     row:
   Short, night, to-night, and length thyself to-mor-
     row.

8 nill: *will not*   conster: *construe*   whether: *which of the two*
14 *Cf. n.*   27 moon: *month*
30 Short: *shorten*   length: *lengthen*

Sonnets to Sundry Notes of Music

I.

It was a lording's daughter, the fairest one of three,
That liked of her master as well as well might be,
Till looking on an Englishman, the fair'st that eye
    could see,
  Her fancy fell a-turning.   4

Long was the combat doubtful that love with love did
    fight,
To leave the master loveless, or kill the gallant knight:
To put in practice either, alas! it was a spite
  Unto the silly damsel.   8

But one must be refused; more mickle was the pain
That nothing could be used to turn them both to gain,
For of the two the trusty knight was wounded with
    disdain:
  Alas! she could not help it.   12

Thus art with arms contending was victor of the day,
Which by a gift of learning did bear the maid away;
Then lullaby, the learned man hath got the lady gay;
  For now my song is ended.   16

II.

On a day, alack the day!
Love, whose month was ever May,
Spied a blossom passing fair,
Playing in the wanton air: 4
Through the velvet leaves the wind,

I. *Cf. n.*   1 lording: *nobleman*
2 master: *teacher*   II. *Cf. n.*

All unseen, 'gan passage find;
That the lover, sick to death,
Wish'd himself the heaven's breath.   8
'Air,' quoth he, 'thy cheeks may blow;
Air, would I might triumph so!
But, alas! my hand hath sworn
Ne'er to pluck thee from thy thorn: 12
Vow, alack! for youth unmeet:
Youth, so apt to pluck a sweet.
Thou for whom Jove would swear
Juno but an Ethiop were;   16
And deny himself for Jove,
Turning mortal for thy love.'

III.

My flocks feed not,
My ewes breed not,
My rams speed not,
    All is amiss: 4
Love's denying,
Faith's defying,
Heart's renying,
    Causer of this.   8
All my merry jigs are quite forgot,
All my lady's love is lost, God wot:
Where her faith was firmly fix'd in love,
There a nay is plac'd without remove.   12
One silly cross
Wrought all my loss;
    O frowning Fortune! cursed, fickle dame;
For now I see   16
Inconstancy
    More in women than in men remain.

III. *Cf. n.*
7 renying: *abjuring*   6 defying: *rejecting*

In black mourn I,
All fears scorn I,   20
Love hath forlorn me,
  Living in thrall:
Heart is bleeding,
All help needing,   24
O cruel speeding,
  Fraughted with gall!
My shepherd's pipe can sound no deal,
My wether's bell rings doleful knell;   28
My curtal dog, that wont to have play'd,
Plays not at all, but seems afraid;
My sighs so deep
Procure to weep,   32
  In howling wise, to see my doleful plight.
How sighs resound
Through heartless ground,
  Like a thousand vanquish'd men in bloody
    fight!
                                                      36

Clear well spring not,
Sweet birds sing not,
Green plants bring not
  Forth their dye;   40
Herds stand weeping,
Flocks all sleeping,
Nymphs back peeping
  Fearfully: 44
All our pleasure known to us poor swains,
All our merry meetings on the plains,
All our evening sport from us is fled,
All our love is lost, for Love is dead.   48
  Farewell, sweet lass,

26 Fraughted: *freighted*   29 curtal: *having the tail docked*

Thy like ne'er was
    For a sweet content, the cause of all my moan:
Poor Corydon   52
Must live alone;
    Other help for him I see that there is none.

IV.

Whenas thine eye hath chose the dame,
And stall'd the deer that thou should'st strike,
Let reason rule things worthy blame,
As well as fancy, partial wight: 4
    Take counsel of some wiser head,
    Neither too young nor yet unwed.

And when thou com'st thy tale to tell,
Smooth not thy tongue with filed talk,   8
Lest she some subtle practice smell;
A cripple soon can find a halt:
    But plainly say thou lov'st her well,
    And set thy person forth to sell.   12

What though her frowning brows be bent,
Her cloudy looks will clear ere night;
And then too late she will repent
That thus dissembled her delight;   16
    And twice desire, ere it be day,
    That which with scorn she put away.

What though she strive to try her strength,
And ban and brawl, and say thee nay,   20
Her feeble force will yield at length,
When craft hath taught her thus to say,
    'Had women been so strong as men,
    In faith, you had not had it then.'   24

IV. *Cf. n.*   2 stall'd: *brought to a standstill*
8 filed: *polished*

And to her will frame all thy ways;
Spare not to spend, and chiefly there
Where thy desert may merit praise,
By ringing in thy lady's ear: 28
    The strongest castle, tower, and town,
    The golden bullet beats it down.

Serve always with assured trust,
And in thy suit be humble true;   32
Unless thy lady prove unjust,
Seek never thou to choose anew.
    When time shall serve, be thou not slack
    To proffer, though she put thee back.   36

The wiles and guiles that women work,
Dissembled with an outward show,
The tricks and toys that in them lurk,
The cock that treads them shall not know.   40
    Have you not heard it said full oft,
    A woman's nay doth stand for nought?

Think, women love to match with men
And not to live so like a saint: 44
Here is no heaven; they holy then
Begin when age doth them attaint.
    Were kisses all the joys in bed,
    One woman would another wed.   48

But, soft! enough! too much, I fear;
For if my mistress hear my song,
She will not stick to round me on th' ear
To teach my tongue to be so long: 52
    Yet will she blush, here be it said,
    To hear her secrets so bewray'd.

51 round: *whisper* (?)

V.

Live with me, and be my love,
And we will all the pleasures prove
That hills and valleys, dales and fields,
And all the craggy mountains yields.   4

There will we sit upon the rocks,
And see the shepherds feed their flocks,
By shallow rivers, by whose falls
Melodious birds sing madrigals.   8

There will I make thee a bed of roses,
With a thousand fragrant posies,
A cap of flowers, and a kirtle
Embroider'd all with leaves of myrtle.   12

A belt of straw and ivy buds,
With coral clasps and amber studs;
And if these pleasures may thee move,
Then live with me and be my love.   16

LOVE'S ANSWER.

If that the world and love were young,
And truth in every shepherd's tongue,
These pretty pleasures might me move,
To live with thee and be thy love.   20

VI.

As it fell upon a day
In the merry month of May,
Sitting in a pleasant shade
Which a grove of myrtles made,   4

V. *Cf. n.*
VI. *Cf. n.*

8 madrigals: *ditties*

Beasts did leap, and birds did sing,
Trees did grow, and plants did spring;
Everything did banish moan,
Save the nightingale alone: 8
She, poor bird, as all forlorn,
Lean'd her breast up-till a thorn,
And there sung the dolefull'st ditty,
That to hear it was great pity: 12
'Fie, fie, fie!' now would she cry;
'Tereu, Tereu!' by and by;
That to hear her so complain,
Scarce I could from tears refrain;   16
For her griefs, so lively shown,
Made me think upon mine own.
Ah! thought I, thou mourn'st in vain,
None takes pity on thy pain: 20
Senseless trees they cannot hear thee,
Ruthless beasts they will not cheer thee:
King Pandion he is dead,
All thy friends are lapp'd in lead,   24
All thy fellow birds do sing
Careless of thy sorrowing.
Even so, poor bird, like thee,
None alive will pity me.   28
Whilst as fickle Fortune smil'd,
Thou and I were both beguil'd.
    Every one that flatters thee
Is no friend in misery.   32
Words are easy, like the wind;
Faithful friends are hard to find:
Every man will be thy friend
Whilst thou hast wherewith to spend;   36
But if store of crowns be scant,

10 up-till: *up against*   23 Pandion; *cf. n.*
24 lapp'd: *wrapped*

No man will supply thy want.
If that one be prodigal,
Bountiful they will him call,   40
And with such-like flattering,
'Pity but he were a king.'
If he be addict to vice,
Quickly him they will entice;   44
If to women he be bent,
They have him at commandement:
But if Fortune once do frown,
Then farewell his great renown;   48
They that fawn'd on him before
Use his company no more.
He that is thy friend indeed,
He will help thee in thy need: 52
If thou sorrow, he will weep;
If thou wake, he cannot sleep:
Thus of every grief in heart
He with thee does bear a part.   56
These are certain signs to know
Faithful friend from flattering foe.

43 addict: *addicted*

A Lover's Complaint

FROM off a hill whose concave womb re-worded
A plaintful story from a sistering vale,
My spirits to attend this double voice accorded,
And down I laid to list the sad-tun'd tale;   4
Ere long espied a fickle maid full pale,
    Tearing of papers, breaking rings a-twain,
    Storming her world with sorrow's wind and rain.

Upon her head a platted hive of straw,   8
Which fortified her visage from the sun,
Whereon the thought might think sometime it saw
The carcass of a beauty spent and done:
Time had not scythed all that youth begun,   12
    Nor youth all quit; but, spite of heaven's fell rage,
    Some beauty peep'd through lattice of sear'd age.

Oft did she heave her napkin to her eyne,
Which on it had conceited characters,   16
Laund'ring the silken figures in the brine
That season'd woe had pelleted in tears,
And often reading what contents it bears;
    As often shrieking undistinguish'd woe   20
    In clamours of all size, both high and low.

Sometimes her levell'd eyes their carriage ride,
As they did battery to the spheres intend;
Sometime diverted, their poor balls are tied   24
To th' orbed earth; sometimes they do extend
Their view right on; anon their gazes lend

2 sistering: *sisterly, neighboring*   4 list: *listen to*
8 platted . . . straw: *head covering of plaited straw*
15 heave: *raise*   napkin: *handkerchief*
17 Laund'ring: *washing*   18 pelleted: *formed into pellets*
22, 23 *Cf. n.*   26 lend; *cf. n.*

To every place at once, and nowhere fix'd,
The mind and sight distractedly commix'd.   28

Her hair, nor loose nor tied in formal plat,
Proclaim'd in her a careless hand of pride;
For some, untuck'd, descended her sheav'd hat,
Hanging her pale and pined cheek beside;   32
Some in her threaden fillet still did bide,
    And true to bondage would not break from thence,
    Though slackly braided in loose negligence.

A thousand favours from a maund she drew   36
Of amber, crystal, and of beaded jet,
Which one by one she in a river threw,
Upon whose weeping margent she was set;
Like usury, applying wet to wet,   40
    Or monarch's hands that lets not bounty fall
    Where want cries some, but where excess begs all.

Of folded schedules had she many a one,
Which she perus'd, sigh'd, tore, and gave the flood; 44
Crack'd many a ring of posied gold and bone,
Bidding them find their sepulchres in mud;
Found yet moe letters sadly penn'd in blood,
    With sleided silk feat and affectedly   48
    Enswath'd, and seal'd to curious secrecy.

These often bath'd she in her fluxive eyes,
And often kiss'd, and often 'gan to tear;
Cried 'O false blood! thou register of lies,   52
What unapproved witness dost thou bear!
Ink would have seem'd more black and damned here.'

31 sheav'd: *made of straw*   36 maund: *hand-basket*
45 posied: *bearing a motto*   48, 49 *Cf. n.*
48 sleided: *sleaved, i.e. separated into filaments*   feat: *neatly*
    affectedly: *with overmuch curiosity*
50 fluxive: *flowing*

This said, in top of rage the lines she rents,
Big discontent so breaking their contents.   56

A reverend man that graz'd his cattle nigh—
Sometime a blusterer, that the ruffle knew
Of court, of city, and had let go by
The swiftest hours, observed as they flew—   60
Towards this afflicted fancy fastly drew;
   And, privileg'd by age, desires to know
   In brief the grounds and motives of her woe.

So slides he down upon his grained bat,   64
And comely-distant sits he by her side;
When he again desires her, being sat,
Her grievance with his hearing to divide:
If that from him there may be aught applied   68
   Which may her suffering ecstasy assuage,
   'Tis promis'd in the charity of age.

'Father,' she says, 'though in me you behold
The injury of many a blasting hour,   72
Let it not tell your judgment I am old;
Not age, but sorrow, over me hath power:
I might as yet have been a spreading flower,
   Fresh to myself, if I had self-applied   76
   Love to myself and to no love beside.

'But woe is me! too early I attended
A youthful suit—it was to gain my grace—
Of one by nature's outwards so commended,   80
That maidens' eyes stuck over all his face.
Love lack'd a dwelling, and made him her place;
   And when in his fair parts she did abide,
   She was new lodg'd and newly deified.   84

58 ruffle: *turmoil*   61 fancy: *love-sick maid*
64 grained: *rough*   bat: *staff*   69 ecstasy: *transport*

'His browny locks did hang in crooked curls,
And every light occasion of the wind
Upon his lips their silken parcels hurls.
What's sweet to do, to do will aptly find: 88
Each eye that saw him did enchant the mind,
    For on his visage was in little drawn
    What largeness thinks in Paradise was sawn.

'Small show of man was yet upon his chin;   92
His phœnix down began but to appear
Like unshorn velvet on that termless skin
Whose bare out-bragg'd the web it seem'd to wear;
Yet show'd his visage by that cost more dear,   96
    And nice affections wavering stood in doubt
    If best were as it was, or best without.

'His qualities were beauteous as his form,
For maiden-tongu'd he was, and thereof free;   100
Yet, if men mov'd him, was he such a storm
As oft 'twixt May and April is to see,
When winds breathe sweet, unruly though they be.
    His rudeness so with his authoriz'd youth   104
    Did livery falseness in a pride of truth.

'Well could he ride, and often men would say
"That horse his mettle from his rider takes:
Proud of subjection, noble by the sway,   108
What rounds, what bounds, what course, what stop he
    makes!"
And controversy hence a question takes,
    Whether the horse by him became his deed,
    Or he his manage by the well-doing steed.   112

---

91 sawn: *sown*   94 termless: *indescribable*
95 bare: *nudity*   105 livery: *clothe in a livery*
109 rounds, bounds, course, stop; *cf. n.*   111, 112 *Cf. n.*

'But quickly on this side the verdict went:
His real habitude gave life and grace
To appertainings and to ornament,
Accomplish'd in himself, not in his case: 116
All aids, themselves made fairer by their place,
　　Came for additions; yet their purpos'd trim
　　Piec'd not his grace, but were all grac'd by him.

'So on the tip of his subduing tongue   120
All kind of arguments and question deep,
All replication prompt, and reason strong,
For his advantage still did wake and sleep:
To make the weeper laugh, the laugher weep,   124
　　He had the dialect and different skill,
　　Catching all passions in his craft of will:

'That he did in the general bosom reign
Of young, of old; and sexes both enchanted,   128
To dwell with him in thoughts, or to remain
In personal duty, following where he haunted:
Consents bewitch'd, ere he desire, have granted;
　　And dialogu'd for him what he would say,   132
　　Ask'd their own wills, and made their wills obey.

'Many there were that did his picture get,
To serve their eyes, and in it put their mind;
Like fools that in the imagination set   136
The goodly objects which abroad they find
Of lands and mansions, theirs in thought assign'd;
　　And labouring in more pleasures to bestow them
　　Than the true gouty landlord which doth owe
　　them.   140

114 habitude: *disposition*   115 appertainings: *belongings*
118 additions: *marks of distinction*
127 in the general bosom: *in all the bosoms*
132 dialogu'd: *expressed*   140 owe: *possess*

'So many have, that never touch'd his hand,
Sweetly suppos'd them mistress of his heart.
My woeful self, that did in freedom stand,
And was my own fee-simple, not in part,   144
What with his art in youth, and youth in art,
 Threw my affections in his charmed power,
 Reserv'd the stalk and gave him all my flower.

'Yet did I not, as some my equals did,   148
Demand of him, nor being desired yielded;
Finding myself in honour so forbid,
With safest distance I mine honour shielded.
Experience for me many bulwarks builded   152
 Of proofs new-bleeding, which remain'd the foil
 Of this false jewel, and his amorous spoil.

'But, ah! who ever shunn'd by precedent
The destin'd ill she must herself assay?   156
Or forc'd examples, 'gainst her own content,
To put the by-pass'd perils in her way?
Counsel may stop awhile what will not stay;
 For when we rage, advice is often seen   160
 By blunting us to make our wits more keen.

'Nor gives it satisfaction to our blood,
That we must curb it upon others' proof;
To be forbid the sweets that seem so good,   164
For fear of harms that preach in our behoof.
O appetite! from judgment stand aloof;
 The one a palate hath that needs will taste,
 Though Reason weep, and cry "It is thy last."   168

'For further I could say "This man's untrue,"
And knew the patterns of his foul beguiling;

144 my own fee-simple; *cf. n.*   153 foil; *cf. n.*
157, 158 *Cf. n.*

Heard where his plants in others' orchards grew,
Saw how deceits were gilded in his smiling;   172
Knew vows were ever brokers to defiling;
    Thought characters and words merely but art,
    And bastards of his foul adulterate heart.

'And long upon these terms I held my city,   176
Till thus he 'gan besiege me: "Gentle maid,
Have of my suffering youth some feeling pity,
And be not of my holy vows afraid:
That's to ye sworn to none was ever said;   180
    For feasts of love I have been call'd unto,
    Till now did ne'er invite, nor never woo.

' "All my offences that abroad you see
Are errors of the blood, none of the mind;   184
Love made them not: with acture they may be,
Where neither party is nor true nor kind:
They sought their shame that so their shame did
     find,
    And so much less of shame in me remains,   188
    By how much of me their reproach contains.

' "Among the many that mine eyes have seen,
Not one whose flame my heart so much as warm'd,
Or my affection put to the smallest teen,   192
Or any of my leisures ever charm'd:
Harm have I done to them, but ne'er was harm'd;
    Kept hearts in liveries, but mine own was free,
    And reign'd, commanding in his monarchy.   196

' "Look here, what tributes wounded fancies sent me,
Of pallid pearls and rubies red as blood;
Figuring that they their passions likewise lent me

180 That's: *that which is*   185 acture: *action*
192 teen: *sorrow*

Of grief and blushes, aptly understood,   200
In bloodless white and the encrimson'd mood;
   Effects of terror and dear modesty,
   Encamp'd in hearts, but fighting outwardly.

' "And, lo! behold these talents of their hair,   204
With twisted metal amorously impleach'd,
I have receiv'd from many a several fair,
Their kind acceptance weepingly beseech'd,
With th'annexions of fair gems enrich'd,   208
   And deep-brain'd sonnets, that did amplify
   Each stone's dear nature, worth, and quality.

' "The diamond; why, 'twas beautiful and hard,
Whereto his invis'd properties did tend;   212
The deep-green emerald, in whose fresh regard
Weak sights their sickly radiance do amend;
The heaven-hu'd sapphire and the opal blend
   With objects manifold: each several stone,   216
   With wit well blazon'd, smil'd or made some moan.

' "Lo! all these trophies of affections hot,
Of pensiv'd and subdu'd desires the tender,
Nature hath charg'd me that I hoard them not,   220
But yield them up where I myself must render,
That is, to you, my origin and ender;
   For these, of force, must your oblations be,
   Since I their altar, you enpatron me.   224

' "O, then, advance of yours that phraseless hand,   225
Whose white weighs down the airy scale of praise;

204 talents: *riches*	205 impleach'd: *intertwined*
210 nature: *properties*	212 invis'd: *invisible*
215 blend: *blended*	217 blazon'd: *explained*
219 tender: *offer*	221 render: *surrender*
224 *Cf. n.*	225 phraseless: *above praise*

Take all these similes to your own command,
Hallow'd with sighs that burning lungs did raise; 228
What me, your minister, for you obeys,
　　Works under you; and to your audit comes
　　Their distract parcels in combined sums.

' "Lo! this device was sent me from a nun, 232
Or sister sanctified, of holiest note;
Which late her noble suit in court did shun,
Whose rarest havings made the blossoms dote;
For she was sought by spirits of richest coat, 236
　　But kept cold distance, and did thence remove,
　　To spend her living in eternal love.

' "But, O my sweet! what labour is 't to leave
The thing we have not, mastering what not strives, 240
Paling the place which did no form receive,
Playing patient sports in unconstrained gyves?
She that her fame so to herself contrives,
　　The scars of battle 'scapeth by the flight, 244
　　And makes her absence valiant, not her might.

' "O, pardon me, in that my boast is true;
The accident which brought me to her eye
Upon the moment did her force subdue, 248
And now she would the caged cloister fly;
Religious love put out religion's eye:
　　Not to be tempted, would she be immur'd,
　　And now, to tempt, all liberty procur'd. 252

' "How mighty then you are! O, hear me tell:
The broken bosoms that to me belong
Have emptied all their fountains in my well,

229, 230 *Cf. n.*　　　　　　　　　　231 distract: *separated*
234 *Cf. n.*　　　　　　　　　　　235 blossoms; *cf. n.*
236 coat: *coat of arms*　　　241 *Cf. n.*　　　251, 252 *Cf. n.*

And mine I pour your ocean all among: 256
I strong o'er them, and you o'er me being strong,
   Must for your victory us all congest,
   As compound love to physic your cold breast.

' "My parts had power to charm a sacred nun,   260
Who, disciplin'd, ay, dieted in grace,
Believ'd her eyes when they t' assail begun,
All vows and consecrations giving place.
O most potential love! vow, bond, nor space,   264
   In thee hath neither sting, knot, nor confine,
   For thou art all, and all things else are thine.

' "When thou impressest, what are precepts worth
Of stale example? When thou wilt inflame,   268
How coldly those impediments stand forth
Of wealth, of filial fear, law, kindred, fame!
Love's arms are peace, 'gainst rule, 'gainst sense,
     'gainst shame,
   And sweetens, in the suffering pangs it bears,   272
   The aloes of all forces, shocks, and fears.

' "Now all these hearts that do on mine depend,
Feeling it break, with bleeding groans they pine;
And supplicant their sighs to you extend,   276
To leave the battery that you make 'gainst mine,
Lending soft audience to my sweet design,
   And credent soul to that strong-bonded oath
   That shall prefer and undertake my troth."   280

'This said, his watery eyes he did dismount,
Whose sights till then were levell'd on my face;
Each cheek a river running from a fount

258 congest: *bring together*   273 aloes: *i.e. bitter experiences*
276 supplicant: *entreating*   279 credent: *believing*
280 prefer: *present*

With brinish current downward flow'd apace.   284
O how the channel to the stream gave grace,
   Who glaz'd with crystal gate the glowing roses
   That flame through water which their hue encloses.

'O father! what a hell of witchcraft lies   288
In the small orb of one particular tear,
But with the inundation of the eyes
What rocky heart to water will not wear?
What breast so cold that is not warmed here?   292
   O cleft effect! cold modesty, hot wrath,
   Both fire from hence and chill extincture hath.

'For, lo! his passion, but an art of craft,
Even there resolv'd my reason into tears;   296
There my white stole of chastity I daft,
Shook off my sober guards and civil fears;
Appear to him, as he to me appears,
   All melting; though our drops this difference
     bore,   300
   His poison'd me, and mine did him restore.

'In him a plenitude of subtle matter,
Applied to cautels, all strange forms receives,
Of burning blushes, or of weeping water,   304
Or swounding paleness; and he takes and leaves,
In either's aptness, as it best deceives,
   To blush at speeches rank, to weep at woes,
   Or to turn white and swound at tragic shows: 308

'That not a heart which in his level came
Could scape the hail of his all-hurting aim,
Showing fair nature is both kind and tame;

293 cleft effect: *twofold result*   294 extincture: *extinction*
297 daft: *doffed, put off*   303 cautels: *wiles*
309 in his level: *within his range of fire*

And, veil'd in them, did win whom he would maim: 312
Against the thing he sought he would exclaim;
  When he most burn'd in heart-wish'd luxury,
  He preach'd pure maid, and prais'd cold chastity.

'Thus merely with the garment of a Grace 316
The naked and concealed fiend he cover'd;
That the unexperient gave the tempter place,
Which like a cherubin above them hover'd.
Who, young and simple, would not be so lover'd? 320
  Ay me! I fell; and yet do question make
  What I should do again for such a sake.

'O that infected moisture of his eye,
O that false fire which in his cheek so glow'd, 324
O that forc'd thunder from his heart did fly,
O that sad breath his spongy lungs bestow'd,
O all that borrow'd motion seeming ow'd,
  Would yet again betray the fore-betray'd, 328
  And new pervert a reconciled maid!'

318 unexperient: *inexperienced*
327 seeming ow'd: *seemingly his own*

FINIS.

NOTES

Epigraph. From Ovid, *Amores*, I. El. xv, 35-36. It is printed on the title page of the original edition. Thus translated by Marlowe: 'Let base conceited wits admire vile things/Fair Phœbus lead me to the Muses' springs.'

Dedicatory Epistle. Henry Wriothesley. Third Earl of Southampton (1573-1624), Shakespeare's patron. He is generally identified with the friend to whom Shakespeare addressed his *Sonnets*.

3. *Rose-cheek'd.* This expression is to be found in Marlowe's *Hero and Leander* (l. 93).

9. *Stain.* In Elizabethan English the word often meant: 'to surpass,' 'to shame.' Cf. *Romeus and Juliet* (Shaks. Soc. 77): 'Whose beauty and whose shape so far the rest did stain.' Here used as a noun: the nymphs looked mean compared to Adonis.

11. *Nature that made thee, with herself at strife.* Nature vied with herself when she created Adonis.

12. *the world hath ending with thy life.* Should Adonis die, Nature would cease to create other beings.

25. *sweating palm.* A moist palm was supposed to be the indication of an amorous disposition (cf., further, l. 143, and *Othello*, III. iv. 36-38), whilst a dry hand meant indifference to love.

53. *miss.* I.e. misdeed. A more usual form was 'amiss.' On this line, cf. *Notes and Queries*, 10th Ser., vol. IX (1908), pp. 264, 506.

56. *Tires.* A term of falconry, especially used of hawks tearing their food (from French *tirer,* to pull).

61. *Forc'd to content.* Adonis is obliged to bear contentedly what he cannot avoid.

71. *rank.* Often applied to an overflowing river. Cf. *King John,* V. iv. 54.

82. *Till he take truce with her contending tears.* Till he cease to resist the assault of tears.

86. *dive-dapper.* A small water-fowl of the Grebe kind, also called dab-chick or dip-chick.

104. *uncontrolled crest.* The crest was properly the feathers on the top of a helmet, here used for the helmet itself. Shakespeare means that Mars had never bowed his head before a victorious enemy.

129-132. *Make . . . time.* Cf. Ovid, *Ars Am.,* III, 59-80.

130. *Beauty . . . wasted.* Cf. Shakespeare's *Sonnets,* I-VI.

158. *Can thy right hand seize love upon thy left.* A way of saying that Adonis is in love with himself.

161. *Narcissus.* Shakespeare's Adonis has several traits in common with Narcissus.

197, 198. *And were . . . sun.* If Venus were not immortal, she would be consumed between the heavenly fire (the sun) and the earthly fire (Adonis).

203, 204. *O, had . . . unkind.* An allusion to Myrrha, Adonis's mother. Cf. Appendix A, p. 172.

231. *deer.* A play upon the words 'deer' and 'dear.'

235. *relief.* Not 'food,' as is generally explained, but 'relievo,' said in topography of all prominence above the ground plan. Cf., further, 'bottom-grass,' 'plain,' 'hillocks.' It was a common-place metaphor in Shakespeare's time.

240. *rouse.* I.e. 'drive from cover.' A term used in venery, generally applied to the hart or the deer. But Shakespeare loosely uses it for sundry sorts of animals, and even for the owl (cf. *Twelfth Night,* II. iii. 60).

247. *Caves.* I.e. the dimples on Adonis's cheeks.

259-262. Shakespeare may have derived the idea of this passage from Ovid, *Ars Am.,* II, 487-488: 'In

furias agitantur equae spatioque remota/Per loca
dividuos amne sequuntur equos.'

263, 264. Cf. Marlowe, *Hero and Leander:* 'For as
a hot proud horse highly disdains/To have his head
controll'd, but breaks the reins,/Spits forth the ringled
bit, and with his hoves/Checks the submissive ground.'

279. *Curvets.* A term of the *manege* or science of
equitation. A 'curvet' is a movement made by a horse,
when he raises his fore legs together, and then, while
he is bringing them down, raises his hind legs without
touching the ground.

286. *Caparisons or trapping.* Richly embroidered
dresses and embellishments used in decorating horses,
especially in tourneys and jousts.

289-292. Possibly an allusion to Nicon, 'the famous
painter of Greece,' who, according to Topsell (*Four-
footed Beasts,* 222), 'when he had most curiously
limbed a horses perfection, and failed in no part of
nature or art, but only in placing hairs under his
eye, for that only fault he received a disgraceful
blame.' (Quoted by Pooler.)

295-298. *Round-hoofed, etc.* Several sources have
been proposed for the description of the points of a
fine horse: Sylvester's translation of Du Bartas, Blun-
devill's *Arte of Ryding,* Googe's *Foure Bookes of Hus-
bandry,* Topsell's *Four-footed Beasts.* Prof. Carleton
Brown (*The Library,* 3rd Ser., No. 10, vol. III,
182 ff.) has shown that for such descriptions there
was a long literary tradition going back to Roman
and Greek times. Cf. Dodge (Neil), *Modern Phi-
lology,* IX, 211 ff.; Law (R. A.) *Modern Lang. Notes,*
XXVIII, 93.

303. *To bid the wind a base.* He prepares to
challenge the wind to strive for superiority in speed.
From the game 'base' or 'prisoner's base.' 'To bid
base' was a frequent locution. Cf. *Two Gentlemen
of Verona,* I. ii. 97.

329-336. Cf. Lodge, *Glaucus and Scylla:* 'Themis

that knewe that waters long restrained/Breake foorth
with greater billowes than the brookes/That swetely
float through meades with floures distained,/With
cheerefull laies did raise his heavie lookes;/And bad
him speake and tell what him agreev'd:/For griefes
disclos'd (said she) are soone releev'd.'

335. *Heart's attorney.* I.e. the tongue. In *Richard III* (IV. iv. 127) words are compared to 'windy
attorneys to their client woes.'

342. *For all askance he holds her in his eye.* He
looks at her sideways, watching her movements all the
time.

359, 360. These two lines are given as a proof
that the poem was written not at Stratford, but when
Shakespeare was already familiar with the life of the
theatres. A dumb play, or dumb show, was a scene in
a tragedy shown pantomimically and representing
parts of the story which could not be included, or
sometimes giving a summary of the action which was
to follow. *Chorus,* a character in the old English
drama, who presented or commented upon the tragedy.

367. *Engine of her thoughts.* This description of
the tongue occurs also in *Titus Andronicus,* III. i. 82:
'that delightful engine of her thoughts.'

370. *My heart . . . wound.* Were my heart as
whole as thine and thy heart wounded like mine.

375. *steel.* With probably a pun on 'steel'
(harden) and 'steal' (rob).

397. *naked bed.* This expression seems to have
been common in the sixteenth century. Its meaning
has not been satisfactorily explained. Here the phrase
evidently means 'lying naked in bed.'

412. *My love to love is love but to disgrace it.* The
only love I bear to love is a strong inclination to disgrace it.

424. *alarms.* Or alarums, signals by which soldiers were warned to take arms.

433-450. *Had I . . . feast.* Wyndham compares

this passage with Chapman's *Ovid's Banquet of Sense* (1595).

472. *Fair fall the wit.* May prosperity befall the wit, etc.

478. *To mend the hurt that his unkindness marr'd.* 'A mixture of two phrases, (1) to mend the hurt that his unkindness caused, and (2) to mend what was marred by his unkindness, i.e. to restore her consciousness or colour' (Pooler).

482. *windows.* Shakespeare uses the word both in the sense of 'eye' (*Love's Labour's Lost,* V. ii. 846), and of 'eyelid' (*Antony and Cleopatra,* V. ii. 319).

506. *liveries.* A livery (Fr. *livrée*) was the distinctive dress worn by the servants and dependants in the household of a nobleman.

507-510. *their verdure, etc.* 'The poet evidently alludes to a practice of his own age, when it was customary, in time of the plague, to strew the rooms of every house with rue and other strong-smelling herbs, to prevent infection' (Malone). There was an outbreak of the plague in August, 1592, and the infection lasted until the spring of 1594. During most of that time the plays were under restraint and the theatres closed. This allusion has been used as a clue to the date of composition of *Venus and Adonis.*

515. *Slips.* It has been supposed that there is a reference to the sense of 'counterfeit money.' It is true that 'slip' sometimes means a 'counterfeit coin,' but the context shows that here 'slip' is taken in its ordinary sense of 'error.' Adonis is making a purchase, and a deed is, therefore, to be drawn; and for fear there should be some omission or error which might be invoked as a cause of non-execution, Adonis will set his seal (i.e. his lips) to the legal instrument (Venus's lips) as a token of performance (cf. line 521).

516. *wax-red.* The seal was impressed on wax affixed to the document.

529. *the world's comforter.* I.e. the sun. Cf., above, l. 484.

565, 566. Cf. Lyly, *Euphues* (Bond's ed., I, 187): 'The tender youth of a childe is like the temperinge of new wax apt to receive any form.'

589, 590. Cf. Lodge, *Glaucus and Scylla:* 'An yvorie shadowed front, . . ./Next which her cheekes appeerd like crimson silk,/Or ruddie rose bespred on whitest milk.'

598. *Manage.* Or *manege,* a term of horsemanship = to train a horse to graceful motions, 'regere et gubernare, propriè est equisonum qui solent equos refractarios, orisque immorigeri, hoc modo domare, fraenoque obsequentes reddere' (Minsheu).

601. *painted grapes.* An allusion to the anecdote reported of Zeuxis by Pliny: 'Zeuxis for proof of his cunning brought upon the scaffold a table, wherein were clusters of grapes so lively painted, that the very birds of the air flew flocking thither for to be pecking at the grapes' (Holland's Pliny, II, 535).

608. *assay'd . . . prov'd.* These words have the same meaning, that of putting a metal to the test. There is besides a play on the word *prove* = 'to test' and 'to feel.'

615-618. *O be advis'd . . . kill.* Cf. Ovid, *Met.,* X, 544-549; 705-707.

619-630. *On his . . . rushes.* Cf. Ovid, *Met.,* VIII, 284-289; 294-295.

626. *Are better proof than thy spear's point can enter.* Are too strong (as an armor tested) for the point of thy spear to enter.

631. Cf. Ovid, *Met.,* X, 547-548.

652. *Kill, kill.* The cry formerly uttered by the English soldiers when they made an onset.

673-678. *But if . . . hounds.* Cf. Ovid, *Met.,* X, 537-539.

673-708. See Appendix A, p. 174.

683. *Musits,* or musets, are gaps in a hedge through

which the hare is accustomed to pass; also the form where the hare hides (cf. French *musse*).

685-688. *Sometime . . . yell.* Cf. Turberville, *Booke of Hunting* (Clarendon Press ed., 165): 'And I have seen hares oftentimes runne into a flocke of sheepe in the field when they were hunted, and would never leave the flocke, until I was forced to couple up my houndes, and fold up the sheepe or sometimes drive them to the cote; and then the hare would forsake them . . . I have seene that would take the grounde like a coney.' (Quoted by Pooler.)

693, 694. *Till they have singled With much ado the cold fault cleanly out.* Till they have with great difficulty distinguished the scent of the animal they hunt from the scent of other animals and thus have corrected the fault they made (a dog is then said to be 'at fault') in losing the scent.

695. *spend their mouths.* A technical term of the chase, 'give tongue.' The same phrase occurs in *Henry V*, II. iv. 70, and *Troilus and Cressida*, V. i. 100.

696. *As if another chase were in the skies.* Cf. *Titus Andronicus*, II. iii. 17-19.

697-699. *By this . . . still.* When the hare 'hath left both hunters and dogs a great way behinde her, she getteth to some hill or rising of the earth, there she raiseth herself upon her hinder legs, like a watchman in his tower, observing how far or near the enemy approacheth' (Topsell, *Four-footed Beasts,* 211).

701, 702. *And now . . . passing-bell.* When the hare 'can go no more, needs must her weakness betray her to her foe, and so was her flight and want of rest like a sickness begun before her death, and the Foxes presence like the voyce of a passing-bell' (Topsell, *Four-footed Beasts,* 210).

704. *indenting.* Following a meandering course comparable to the indented line in which the duplicates of a legal document were cut out to make them tally with each other. Topsell has (p. 212): 'The dogs run

along with a gallant cry, turning over the doubtful steps; now one way, now another (like the cuts of Indentures, through rough and plain, crooked and straight. . . .'

720. *In night . . . desire sees best of all.* Cf. Marlowe, *Hero and Leander:* 'Dark night is Cupid's day.'

725. *cloudy.* Has here the double meaning of 'covered with clouds' and 'gloomy.'

726. *forsworn.* Since she had vowed to remain chaste.

730. *moulds.* The mould in which Adonis was cast, when he was created.

751. *fruitless chastity.* Cf. Marlowe, *Hero and Leander:* 'A fruitless cold virginity.'

757, 758. *What . . . posterity.* Cf. Sonnet III, 7, 8. Note the strange rime of *posterity'* with *obscúrity.* It is discussed by Neil Dodge, 'An Obsolete Elizabethan Mode of Rhyming,' *Shakespeare Studies* (University of Wisconsin), 1916.

768. *But gold that's put to use more gold begets.* Cf. Marlowe, *Hero and Leander:* 'Then treasure is abused/When misers keep it: being put to loan/In time it will return us two for one.'

828. *discovery.* Adonis has just been compared (l. 815) to a bright star shooting from the sky; Venus, therefore, remains 'confounded' in the dark, having lost the fair light which might have helped her to find out her way.

848. *parasites.* Those sounds being but echoes to her lamentations seem to flatter her obsequiously.

854. *cabinet.* A diminutive of 'cabin,' a small hut. On this line cf. *Notes and Queries,* 10th Ser., vol. V (January-June, 1906), p. 465; vol. IX (1908), p. 505; vol. X, p. 166.

877. *at a bay.* (French *aux abois*), a term of venery, said of the hounds when they have hunted down their game and bay at it; the expression is also used

of the hunted animal when it is obliged to stop and face the hounds.

883, 884. *For now . . . proud.* Cf. Ovid, *Met.*, X, 539-541.

888. *strain courtesy.* The expression means either 'exhibit courtesy reluctantly,' 'fall short of courtesy,' or, on the contrary, 'to be courteous beyond the proper extent.' Here the latter meaning is preferable. Each dog displays an eagerness to let the others go first.

889. *cry.* A term of venery, used of the hounds when they bay. Cf. 'full cry.'

891, 892. *Who, overcome, etc.* 'Her heart overwhelmed with fears withdraws the blood from the limbs, and they in turn refuse their office' (Pooler).

920. *flap-mouth'd.* Having loose, hanging-down lips,—a characteristic point in a swift hound.

933. *worm.* Some commentators give to the word the meaning of 'serpent,' which it sometimes has in Elizabethan English. But is not death naturally associated with the idea of worms?

947. *golden arrow.* Cupid was supposed to have golden arrows to inspire love and leaden ones for disdained lovers.

993. *call'd him all to naught.* Called him a worthless person.

1013. *trophies.* Monuments erected in memory of some victory.

1027. *lure.* A piece of flesh with feathers attached to it, in manner of a bird, used by falconers to recall (or reclaim) a hawk.

1028. *The grass stoops not, she treads on it so light.* Cf. Virgil, *Æneid*, VII, 808-809: 'Illa vel intactae segetis per summa volaret/Gramina nec teneras cursu læsisset aristas.'

1064. *That her sight dazzling makes the wound seem three.* Cf. *3 Henry VI*, II. i. 25: 'Dazzle mine eyes, or do I see three suns?'

1110. *He thought . . . him so.* Malone compares

this passage with a poem 'De Adoni ab apro inter-
empto,' by Minturno, in which the wound made by the
boar is represented as an awkwardly given kiss: 'In-
gens me miserum libido capit/Mille suavia dulcia hinc
capere,/Atque me impulit ingens indomitus.' The
idea is from Theocritus.

1115, 1116. *And nuzzling, etc.* Cf. Ovid, *Met.*, X,
715, 716.

1127. *Coffer-lids.* Or lids to coffers, treasure-
chests. Possibly cover-lid, or coverlet (French *cou-
vrelit,* the covering of a bed).

1148. *Measures.* A dance, more particularly a
stately kind of dance with slow, measured steps. Cf.
Much Ado, II. i. 80, 81, where it is said to be 'man-
nerly-modest' and 'full of state and ancientry.'

1168. *Purple flower.* According to the legend,
Adonis was metamorphosed to an anemone, also called
Adonis. Cf. Ovid, *Met.*, X, 731-739.

1193. *Paphos.* A city on the west coast of Cyprus.
Venus was said to have landed there when she was
born from the sea foam.

LUCRECE

THE ARGUMENT

1-8. It is to be noted that the poem contains noth-
ing corresponding to this part of the argument.

1. *Lucius Tarquinius . . . Superbus.* The last leg-
endary king of Rome (534-510 B.C.). His tyrannical
ways and the outrage of his son upon Lucretia caused
the people to revolt and led to the expulsion of the
Tarquins.

8. *Ardea.* An ancient city of Latium, about twenty-
four miles south of Rome, one of the most wealthy in
that part of Italy.

12. *Collatinus.* L. Tarquinius, the son of Egerius,

resided in the town of Collatia; hence his surname of Collatinus. He was cousin to Tarquinius Superbus, and after the dethronement of the latter he was elected one of the consuls.

31. *dispatcheth messengers, etc.* In the poem, Lucrece sends only one messenger, to her husband.

34. *Junius Brutus.* Lucius Junius, after his father's death, to escape being murdered by Tarquinius Superbus, feigned madness, whence his surname of Brutus.

34. *Publius Valerius.* Surnamed Publicola. He took a prominent part in the dethronement of the Tarquins and was the colleague of Brutus in the consulship.

4. *Collatium.* I.e. Collatia, a city of Latium, about ten miles east of Rome.

8, 9. *Haply . . . appetite.* Wyndham compares Ovid, *Fasti*, ii, 765: 'Verba placent, et vox, et quod corrumpere non est:/Quoque minor spes est, hoc magis ille cupit.' But Shakespeare's text is nearer Livy's: 'Cum forma tum spectata castitas incitat.'

14. *aspects.* The position of the stars or planets with respect to one another.

26. *An expir'd date, cancell'd ere well begun.* Cf. Daniel, *Rosamonde* (249): 'Cancelled with Time, will have their date expired.'

47. *liver.* In Shakespeare's days, the liver was supposed to be the seat of love or desire. Cf. *Much Ado*, IV. i. 233: 'If ever love had interest in his liver.' Also, *Twelfth Night*, II. iv. 101.

49. *spring.* Two meanings are possible: 1, a too early spring is blighted by the cold and cannot grow old; 2, premature shoots (springs) are blighted by the cold and therefore cannot grow. The former is preferable.

52-70. *Within whose face beauty and virtue striv'd, etc.* This passage describes the contention

between Beauty and Virtue in terms of heraldry, red
being identified with 'or' or gold and white with silver
(more properly 'argent'), two of the metals employed
in blazonry. The sense can be paraphrased as fol-
lows: At sight of Tarquin, Lucrece changed color
several times, her cheeks being by turns red and white
(cf. ll. 257-259). When Virtue, whose color is
white, appeared to be dominant (bragged), Beauty
blushed; but, then, Virtue was jealous and tried to
surpass (stain) the 'or' of those blushes with the silver
of her paleness. Beauty, who considered she had a
right (intituled) to white, then claimed a field silver
from Venus's doves. As a retort, Virtue claimed
Beauty's red, to which she had also a right, for she
had given it to the golden age that men, in that virtu-
ous age, might display it combined with silver on their
shield, the shield being to be used as a defensive armor
when shame assailed.

67. *minority*. Cf. 'golden age' at l. 60. From the
days when the world was still young, Beauty and Vir-
tue have thus asserted their rights.

72. *field*. A play on the double meaning of the
word: 1, field, heraldic term; 2, field of battle.

82. *owe*. Because he had been a niggard in his
praise he had not given the full sum of commendation
which he ought to have paid.

88. *lim'd*. Caught by bird-lime. Steevens appo-
sitely cites *3 Henry VI*, V. vi. 13: 'The bird that hath
been limed in a bush/With trembling wings mis-
doubteth every bush.'

104, 105. *Nor . . . light*. 'Lucrece could see that
Tarquin was looking, but not what his looks meant'
(Pooler).

106-112. *He stories, etc.* Gower (*Confessio Aman-
tis*) also makes Collatinus the subject of Tarquin's
conversation with Lucrece.

117-119. *Till sable . . . Day*. Cf. Daniel, *Rosa-
monde:* 'Night (mother of sleepe and feare)/Who with

her sable mantle friendly covers/The sweet-stolne
sport of ioyfull meeting lovers' (439).

120-123. *For . . . questioned.* Cf. Livy: 'Cum
post cenam in hospitale cubiculum deductus esset.'

135, 136. *That what, etc.* This passage has been
much emended. Quartos 5 to 8 have 'That oft, what';
Staunton conjectured 'For what'; Nicholson, 'That
while.' The quarto reading, though not very clear,
yields, however, an acceptable sense: Those that covet
much are so foolish that they scatter what they have
not as well as that which they possess, for in their
hope to get more they spend beyond their power.

138-140. *Or, gaining more, etc.* If they succeed in
getting more, all their profit is but to have more than
is necessary, and to experience the griefs that go with
fortune, so that, in the end, in this valueless gain they
really are bankrupt.

150-152. *And this . . . we have.* 'Rich men suf-
fering from the disease of ambition are tortured by the
thought that they are destitute of what they have, viz.
abundance' (Pooler).

187, 188. *Then looking . . . lust.* 'He despises
his naked or defenceless protection from Lust, now
still and slaughtered by Fear' (Wyndham).

197-210. Cf. Chaucer, *Legend of Good Women*
(1822-1824): 'Why hastow doon dispite to chevalrye?/
Why hastow doon thys lady vylanye?/Allas, of the
thys was a vilenous deede!'

206, 207. *Some loathsome . . . dote.* In heraldry
there exist special marks of disgrace, called 'abate-
ments,' to denote some 'ungentleman-like, dishonor-
able, disloyal demeanour, quality or stain in the bearer,
whereby the dignity of the Coat-armour' is 'greatly
abased' (Guillim, *Display of Heraldry*). They con-
sist of 'diminution and reversing; the first is the
blemishing some particular point of the escutcheons
by sanguine and tenny [orange], which are stains.
Reversing signifies some parts of the charge backward

or upside down' (Pinnock's *Catechism of Heraldry*). The figures used for 'abatements of honour' were not of metal, but 'tinged or coloured' either tenny or sanguine.

245. *painted cloth.* Pieces of canvas painted in oil and used for hangings in Elizabethan houses. They were often painted with Scripture incidents and ornamented with mottoes or moral sentences. (Cf. *1 Henry IV*, IV. ii. 28; *Troilus and Cressida*, V. x. 46.)

265. *Narcissus.* Cf. note on *Venus and Adonis*, 161.

278. *My part is youth, and beats these from the stage.* Probably an allusion to some morality play—such as *Lusty Juventus*—now lost.

318. *rushes.* In old days it was customary to strew the rooms with rushes for carpets.

341. *So from himself impiety hath wrought.* 'His sin has made him so unlike himself' (Pooler).

342. *Prey to pray.* 'A jingle not less disgusting occurs in Ovid's narrative of the same event (*Fasti*, ii, 787) "Hostis, ut hospes, init penetralia Collatina" ' (Steevens).

356. *eye of Heaven.* The sun. Cf. *Richard II*, I. iii. 275; III. ii. 37.

365. *stalks.* So Chaucer, *Legend of Good Women* (l. 1781): 'And in the night ful thefely gan he stalke.'

386-395. *Her lily hand, etc.* Sir John Suckling has a poem entitled 'A Supplement of an imperfect copy of verses of Mr Wil. Shakespears' (ed. W. C. Hazlitt, I, 27), the first lines of which are, with certain variants, lines 386-395 of Shakespeare's *Lucrece*. The beginning of the poem runs as follows:

One of her hands, one of her cheeks lay under,
 Cozening the pillow of a lawful kisse,
Which therefore swel'd and seem'd to part asunder,
 As angry to be rob'd of such a blisse:
  The one lookt pale, and for revenge did long,
  Whilst t'other blush't, cause it had done the wrong.

2

Out of the bed the other fair hand was
  On a green satin quilt, whose perfect white
Lookt like a Dazie in a field of grasse
  [1]And shewed like unmelt snowe unto the sight [1] Thus far
    There lay this pretty perdue, safe to keep   Shakespeare.
    The rest o th'body that lay fast asleep.

As we have no reason to suspect Suckling's statement
that he had an imperfect copy of Shakespeare's verses,
and as several lines differ from the corresponding lines
in the authentic version, we may admit that Shake-
speare had contemplated writing his *Lucrece* in the
six-line stanza of *Venus and Adonis*, but that, for
some unknown reason, after having tried a stanza or
so, he rejected it and adopted the seven-line stanza.
(Cf. B. Nicholson, *Notes and Queries*, 1884, June 7, p.
444.)

397. *marigolds*. The marigold was the emblem of
constancy in affection and was said 'to go to bed with
the sun' (*Winter's Tale*, IV. iv. 105).

400. *golden threads*. Ovid speaks of Lucrece's
'flavi capilli.' Chaucer has 'yellow heer.'

407-409. *Her breasts . . . knew*. Cf. Ovid, *Fasti*,
ii, 803-804: 'positis urguentur pectora palmis,/Tunc
primum externa pectora tacta manu.'

417. *tir'd*. Cf. note on *Venus and Adonis*, 56.

437-439. *His hand . . . breast*. Compare Livy's
'sinistra manu mulieris pectore oppresso' with Ovid's
'positis urguentur pectora palmis.'

459. *antics*. Grotesques, or fantastic forms.

476, 477, 481. *colour*. A play on the different
meanings of the word: pretext, hue, standard.

477-504. Shakespeare may have found the idea of
Tarquin's speech in Livy: 'Tum Tarquinius fateri amo-
rem, orare, miscere precibus minas, versare in omnes
partes muliebrem animum.' Ovid has only: 'Instat
amans hostis precibus pretioque minisque' (805).

477-511. Cf. Ovid, *Fasti,* ii, 803, and Chaucer, *Legend of Good Women,* ll. 1790 ff.

492. *I know what thorns the growing rose defends.* Cf. Daniel, *Rosamonde:* 'The ungather'd Rose defended with the thornes' (217).

509. *falchion.* A play upon the words falchion and falcon (cf. above, l. 506).

511. *falcon's bells.* Falconers fastened bells, often made of silver, to the legs of their hawks or falcons.

522. *nameless bastardy.* Malone compares *Two Gentlemen of Verona,* III. i. 324-326: 'bastard vertues, that indeed know not their fathers, and therefore have no names.'

537. *Worse than a slavish wipe.* 'More disgraceful than the brand with which slaves were marked' (Malone).

540. *cockatrice.* Or basilisk. 'The cockatrice slayeth also all thing that hath life, with breath and with sight. In his sight no fowl nor bird passeth harmless, and though he be far from the fowl, yet it is burnt and devoured by his mouth' (Bartholomew's *De Propriet. rerum,* translated by Trevisa, Bk. xviii, §8).

556. *vulture folly.* Cf. Daniel, *Rosamonde:* 'vulture ambition' (27).

565-567. *She puts . . . speaks.* Steevens compares *Midsummer Night's Dream,* V. i. 96-98: 'Make periods in the midst of sentences,/Throttle their practised accent in their fears,/And in conclusion dumbly have broke off.'

596-630. Cf. Chaucer, *Legend of Good Women* (1819-1821): 'Tarquinius, thou art a Kynges eyre,/And sholdest, as by lynage and by right,/Doon as a lorde and as a verray knyght.'

677. *The wolf hath seiz'd his prey, the poor lamb cries.* Cf. Ovid, *Fasti,* ii, 800: 'Sed tremit ut quondam stabulis deprensa relictis/Parva sub infesto cum jacet agna lupo,' and Chaucer, *Legend,* l. 1798: 'Right as a

wolf that fynt a lamb alone,/To whom shall she com-
pleyne or make mone?'

703. *receipt.* What he has received, as in *Coriola-
nus*, I. i. 118: 'the mutinous parts/That envied his re-
ceipt' (said of the belly).

766. *Black stage.* In the Elizabethan system of
staging they often used black hangings as an appro-
priate setting for tragedies. Cf. *1 Henry VI*, I. i. 1;
Warning for Fair Women, Ind. 74; *Insatiate Coun-
tess* (Marston), IV. v. 4.

828. *crest-wounding.* Bringing dishonor to the
crest. In heraldry the crest is the ornament of a
helmet.

830. *mot.* I.e. motto, a sentence (generally writ-
ten on a scroll) above or under an escutcheon.

850. *toads infect.* 'A toad is a manner venomous
frog, and dwelleth both in water and land . . . his
venom is accounted most cold and stonieth' (Bartholo-
mew, *De Propriet. rerum*, Bk. xviii, §17).

858. *Tantalus.* A legendary king of Lydia, who
was afflicted in Hades with eternal hunger and thirst.

874. *ill-annexed Opportunity.* I.e. opportunity
with its evil adjuncts.

876 ff. *O Opportunity, etc.* All this passage seems
to have been strongly influenced by Spenser's *Fairy
Queen.* Compare, for instance, the personification
of Occasion in Bk. ii, canto iv.

950. *cherish.* Warburton proposed as an emenda-
tion 'tarish' (from French *tarir*), dry up. Other
commentators give to 'springs' the meaning of 'shoots,'
in which case 'cherish' means 'nurture,' 'foster.' But
in the whole passage Time is shown as destroying
everything.

956. *unicorn.* 'It is a beast of an untameable na-
ture' (Topsell, *Four-footed Beasts*, 557). 'An unicorn
is a right cruel beast, and hath that name, for he hath
in the middle of the forehead an horn of four foot

long' (Bartholomew, *De Propriet. rerum,* Bk. xviii, 90).

1054. *badge.* The badge was a piece of cloth or of silver with the arms of a nobleman worn on the left sleeve by his servants or dependents. For 'livery' cf. note on *Venus and Adonis,* 506.

1074. *sable ground.* The ground, or field, is the surface of a shield on which are represented the ensigns armorial composing a coat of arms. 'Sable' is the heraldic term for black.

1079. *Philomel.* A daughter of King Pandion, who, being dishonored by her brother-in-law, Tereus, was metamorphosed into a nightingale (or swallow).

1086. *Revealing day through every cranny spies.* On this line see *Notes and Queries,* 11th Ser., vol. IV (1911), p. 243.

1094. *True grief is fond and testy as a child.* On this line see W. Cairns, in *Literature* (London), July 29, 1899, vol. V, p. 111.

1132. *diapason.* An air sounding in exact concord, i.e. in octaves.

1133. *burthen.* The burden was a musical figure which consisted in repeating the theme throughout the song, in the bass, and continuing when the singer of the air paused. Then it came to mean simply, as here, the bass or undersong.

1134. *descant'st.* 'To descant: to play or sing an air in harmony with a fixed theme' (N.E.D.).

better skill. I.e. with better skill. So Malone and others. But Wyndham explains more subtly: 'Shakespeare, here, as ever, exhibits a complete grasp of technical terms. He makes Lucrece contrast her sad, monotonous accompaniment of groans—humming on Tarquin still—with the treble descant of the nightingale, complaining in a higher register and with more frequent modulations of the wrong wrought her by Tereus, according to Ovid's tale. The one he compares to a single droning base, chiefly in the diapason or lower octave; the other to the "better skill" or more ingenious artifice of a contrapuntal melody scored above it.'

1139. *Who, if it wink, shall thereon fall and die.* I.e. and my heart, if my eye wink, shall fall on the knife and die.

1140. *frets.* Pieces of wire, or wood, fixed on the finger board of guitars and other similar instruments serving to regulate the fingering.

1155. *death reproach's debtor.* Death alone can discharge the debt to infamy and thus acquit Lucrece.

1157. *But with my body my poor soul's pollution.* It would be only adding the pollution of the soul to the pollution of the body.

1188-1190. *So of . . . new-born.* Like the Phœnix which was supposed to rise again from its own ashes.

1196. *thy foe.* Because she has brought shame upon him.

1199. *My soul and body, etc.* The formula usually used at the beginning of a will.

1205. *oversee.* The overseers of a will were persons appointed to see that the intentions of the deceased were correctly carried out. Note the play upon the word at the following line.

1220. *With soft slow tongue, true mark of modesty.* Cf. *Lear,* V. iii. 273, of Cordelia: 'Her voice was ever soft,/Gentle, and low,—an excellent thing in woman.'

1234. *Like ivory conduits coral cisterns filling.* Shakespeare was probably thinking of some fountain. Cf. *As You Like It,* IV. i. 154.

1261. *The precedent whereof in Lucrece view.* Cf. Daniel, *Rosamonde:* 'The president whereof presented to my view' (414).

1261-1267. Cf. Chaucer, *Legend of Good Women* (ll. 1814-1818): 'That, what for fere of sklaundre and drede of dethe,/She lost att ones bothe wytte and brethe;/And in a swowgh she lay, and woxe so ded,/

Men myghten smyten of hir arme or hed,/She feleth
nothinge, neither foule ne feyre.'

1324. *To see sad sights moves more than hear them
told.* Cf. Horace, *Ars Poet.*, 180-181: 'Segnius irri-
tant animos demissa per aurem/Quam quae sunt oculis
subjecta fidelibus.'

1342. *But they, etc.* On this line see *Notes and
Queries*, 1874, May 2, p. 343; June 20, p. 484.

1366 ff. *At last, etc.* In Virgil, *Æneid*, I, 454-493,
Æneas similarly views scenes from the fall of Troy
depicted in a temple at Carthage.

1367. *Painting.* Commentators suppose that
Shakespeare had in mind not a picture but a hanging,
or painted cloth. Nothing in the text bears out such a
supposition.

1436. *Dardan.* An adjective applied to Troy, so
called after Dardanus.

1437. *Simois.* A river which flows from Mount
Ida, and joins the river Scamander in the plain of
Troy.

1450, 1451. *In her . . . reign.* Cf. Daniel, *Rosa-
monde:* 'Reade in my face the ruines of my youth/The
wracke of yeeres upon my aged brow' (253-254).

1501. *wretched image.* I.e. Sinon, a son of Ætinus
(or of Sisyphus). He mutilated himself and allowed
himself to be taken prisoner by the Trojans, in order
to facilitate the introduction of the wooden horse, full
of Greeks, into the city of Troy.

1523. *wildfire.* A pyrotechnical composition, burn-
ing even under water, and analogous to Greek fire.

1525. *And little stars shot from their fixed places.*
Cf. Virgil, *Æneid*, ii, 693-696: 'De caelo lapsa per
umbras/Stella facem ducens multa cum luce cucurrit./
Illam, summa super labentem culmina tecti,/Cerni-
mus.' The whole passage is strongly reminiscent of
the second book of the Æneid.

1526. *their glass.* I.e. the burnished roof of
Priam's palace, which reflected the stars.

1544. *armed to beguild.* So all the quartos, 'be-
guild' having the meaning of 'to cover as with gold.'
Perhaps we should read 'to-beguil'd,' all disguised.

1585. *mourning.* Cf. Ovid, *Fasti*, ii, 817-818:
'Utque vident habitum, quae luctus causa, requirunt/
Cui paret exequias.' Also in Chaucer, *Legend*, ll. 1829
ff., and in Bandello (Bk. ii, nov. XXI). This detail
is not in Livy.

1588. *water-galls.* A watery appearance in the
sky, looked upon as a presage of stormy weather.

1604. *Three times.* Cf. Ovid, *Fasti*, ii, 823: 'Ter
conata loqui, ter destitit.'

1620. *A stranger . . . lay.* Cf. Livy: 'Vestigia
viri alieni in lecto sunt tuo.'

1650. *Scarlet lust.* Tarquin being the judge is
clad in scarlet, hence the epithet is applied to his
lust that plays the part of a witness.

1655, 1656. *Though . . . my mind.* Cf. Livy:
'Ceterum corpus est tantum violatum, animus insons.'
This is not in Ovid.

1660 ff. Cf. the King's lamentations in Daniel's
Rosamonde (ll. 792 ff.).

1672, 1673. *Even . . . draw.* 'His sighs make a
saw, the tool so called, of his sorrows by pushing grief
forwards and drawing it back again; i.e. his sighs
gave him only momentary relief, a repetition of ll.
1663-1666, he sighs away his grief and drinks it up
again' (Pooler).

1689-1691. *Speaking . . . mine.* Cf. Livy: 'Sed
date dextras fidemque, haud impune adultero fore . . .
si vos viri estis, . . . dant ordine omnes fidem.' Ovid
has only: 'Hoc quoque Tarquinio debebimus' (825).

1709, 1710. *With this . . . clears.* Cf. Livy: 'Con-
solantur aegram animi . . . mentem peccare, non cor-
pus.' This is not in Ovid.

1714, 1715. *No, no . . . giving.* Cf. Livy, thus
translated in Paynter's *Palace of Pleasure:* 'As for my
part, though I cleare myself of the offence, my body

shall feel the punishment: for no unchast or ill woman shall hereafter impute no dishonest act to Lucrece.' This is not in Ovid.

1732, 1733. Cf. Ovid, *Fasti* (ii, 833-834): 'Ecce super corpus communia damna gementes/Obliti decoris, virque paterque jacent.'

1745. *rigol.* Generally explained 'circle,' a ring, and compared with *2 Henry IV*, IV. v. 36, where the crown is called 'this golden rigol.' Malone cites Nashe (*Lenten Stuff*): 'the ringol or ringed circle was compact and chalkt out.' But 'ringol' (German, ringel, ring) is not 'rigol.' I am inclined to believe that we have here a word connected with the French 'rigole,' which means a small channel for water, also a rivulet (cf. Low Latin 'rigora,' 'rigulus' and Italian 'rigolo,' scanalatura).

1772-1775. Cf. note to 1732, 1733.

1797. *sorrow's interest.* Wyndham compares Sonnet XXXI: 'How many a holy and obsequious tear/Hath dear religious love stol'n from mine eye/As interest of the dead.'

1809, 1810. *Began . . . to show.* See note on Argument, 34.

1843-1848. *And kissed . . . swore.* Cf. Livy: 'Cultrum deinde Collatino tradit, inde Lucretio ac Valerio, stupentibus miraculo rei, unde novum in Bruti pectore ingenium. Ut præceptum erat, jurant.' This is not in Ovid.

1850, 1851. *They did . . . Rome.* This is neither in Ovid nor in Livy. Chaucer (*Legend*, ll. 1861-1866) has: 'Of hir had al the toun of Rome routhe . . ./And openly let cary her, on a bere/Through al the toun.'

THE PHŒNIX AND THE TURTLE

1. *the bird of loudest lay*. It is possible that Shakespeare was thinking of the crane which Chaucer mentions in *Parlement of Foules* (l. 344), 'the crane, the geaunt, with his trompes soune.'

2. *Arabian tree*. The date-palm (Greek φοῖνιξ) which the bird phœnix occupied, hence its name. Cf. *Tempest*, III. iii. 23.

5. *shrieking harbinger*. The screech-owl, which foretells evil and death. Cf. Chaucer, *Parlement*, l. 342, 'The oule eeke, that of the dethe the bode bringeth.' Cf. *Midsummer Night's Dream*, V. ii. 6-8.

10. *tyrant wing*. I.e. birds of prey. Chaucer, *Parlement*, l. 334, says of the eagle: 'Ther was the tyraunt with his fethers donne.'

15. *death-divining*. It was an ancient belief that the swan sang just before his death. Chaucer, *Parlement*, has: 'The Ialous swan, ayens his deth that singeth.' Cf. *King John*, V. vii. 19-21, and *Othello*, V. ii. 245, 246.

17. *treble-dated crow*. The crow, on account of his black color, was a suitable mourner. The crow was believed to live three times three human lives. 'Cornicum ut secla vetusta/Ter tres aetates humanas garrula vincit/Cornix' (Lucretius, V, 1053). The crow was also symbolic of conjugal concord (cf. Alciati, Emblem 38). Hence his presence among the mourners of the faithful pair.

18, 19. *Thy sable gender . . . tak'st*. Probably an allusion to the notion that the raven does not 'conceive by conjunction of male and female, but rather by a kind of billing at the mouth which Pliny (x, 12) mentions as an opinion of the common people' (Swan's *Speculum Mundi*, 1665, p. 397. Quoted by Halliwell.). Two crows were often represented by emblem writers with their bills fast locked one in the other,

which probably suggested the idea of conceiving by
giving and taking breath.

25-28. *So they loved . . . was slain.* Though the
lovers were two, so complete was their union that they
looked as if they were one in essence; each was dis-
tinct from the other, and yet there was no division
between them; in their love the very notion of number
was annihilated.

29, 30. *Hearts . . . seen.* This stanza develops the
same idea as the preceding one. Though their hearts
were remote, because belonging to two different per-
sons, yet they were united; there was a distance be-
tween them, since remote, but no space, that is, no
division.

32. *But . . . wonder.* 'So extraordinary a phe-
nomenon as "hearts remote" yet "not asunder" would
have excited admiration had it been found anywhere
else except in these two birds. In them it was not
wonderful' (Malone).

33-36. *So . . . mine.* Their love shone so bright
that the turtle could see his right, that is, the love due
to him, all a-blaze in the ardent eyes of the phœnix:
Each was the source of inexhaustible treasure (*mine*)
to the other.

37-40. *Property . . . call'd.* Property is a Latin-
ism, 'proprietas,' peculiar or essential quality. Cf.
Richard II, III. ii. 135: 'Sweet love, I see, changing
his property/Turns to the sourest and most deadly
hate.' 'Property' was appalled to find out that per-
sonality had been destroyed, since each lover's identity
was merged into the other's, and was no longer itself.
There were two names to what was in reality one per-
son; therefore it could neither be said that they were
two, since their nature was the same, nor that they
were one, for in fact there were two distinct persons.

42. *Saw division grow together.* Reason cannot
understand how those which seemed different were
now one.

43-46. *To themselves . . . one.* And yet Reason saw that the lovers were different in themselves, for the elements in their several natures were so strongly compounded or blended that Reason could exclaim: 'In this unity, there is a real duality.'

47, 48. *Love . . . remain.* So that Love is right while Reason, which ought to be right, is wrong—since there remains a union where there should be a division.

THE PASSIONATE PILGRIM

I. This is Shakespeare's Sonnet cxxxviii, with important variant readings.

II. This is Shakespeare's Sonnet cxliv, with minor variations.

11. 'Being both friends to me and also to each other.'

III. From *Love's Labour's Lost,* IV. iii. 60-73. Lines 2, 9, 10, 11, and 14 contain slight differences from the text of the play.

IV. Author unknown.

V. From *Love's Labour's Lost,* IV. ii. 110-123, with certain alterations.

VI. Author unknown. The subject is that of one of the pictures offered to Christopher Sly (*Taming of the Shrew,* Ind., ii. 51): 'We will fetch thee straight Adonis painted by the running brook, and Cytherea all in sedges hid.' Sedge is not 'osier' and one might as well see in that difference a proof that the sonnet is not by the same hand as the one that wrote *The Taming of the Shrew.*

VII. Author unknown.

5. *Damask.* A red color resembling that of the damask rose.

VIII. By Richard Barnfield. Appeared in *Poems: in divers Humors* (1598).

3. *Thee.* In Barnfield's *Poems* the sonnet is addressed 'To his friend Master R. L. in praise of music and poetry.' R. L. has been identified as Richard Linche, author of *Diella* (1596).

5. *Dowland.* John Dowland (?1563-?1626), a lute player. He was also a composer and published *Songes or Ayres of Foure Partes with Tableture for the Lute* (1597); *Lacrymae* (1605), etc.

14. *One knight.* Probably Sir George Carey.

IX. Author unknown. The second line of this sonnet appears to have been inadvertently omitted.

X. Author unknown. Unlike IX and XI, this poem is not on the Venus and Adonis theme.

XI. By Bartholomew Griffin. Appeared in *Fidessa more chaste than kind* (1596). In regard to ll. 9-12, which are different in the *Passionate Pilgrim* and in *Fidessa,* Grosart suggested that they were altered so as to be a closer copy of Venus and Adonis. I believe Dowden is right when he says: 'This is a case of hesitation between two treatments of a sonnet-close, the writer being doubtful whether the turn in the thought should take place at the ninth or at the eleventh line.'

9-12. In Griffin's *Fidessa* these four lines are as follows: 'But he a wayward boy refused the offer/ And ran away, the beauteous queen neglecting/Showing both folly to abuse her proffer/And all his sex of cowardice detecting.'

13. *At this bay.* For this expression see note on *Venus and Adonis,* 877.

XII. Has been ascribed to Thomas Deloney. It occurs, with four additional stanzas, in his *Garland of Good Will,* Pt. III. The first edition known is dated 1604.

XIII. Author unknown.

XIV. Author unknown.

14. Pooler proposes to read: 'My heart doth charge

them watch the morning rise,' which is decidedly an improvement.

SONNETS TO SUNDRY NOTES OF MUSIC

I. Author unknown.

II. From *Love's Labour's Lost*, IV. iii. 101-120. The chief alteration is the omission of two lines which are found in the play. This poem was also reprinted in *England's Helicon*, with the title 'The Passionate Shepherds Song.'

III. Author unknown. Previously published in a Collection of Madrigals by Thomas Weelkes (1597). It occurs also in *England's Helicon*, with the title 'The Unknown Shepherd's Complaint.'

IV. Author unknown. Prof. Dowden, in his Introduction to Griggs' facsimile, seems ready to accept Grosart's suggestion that this poem is somehow connected with *Willobie his Avisa*. All that can be said is that the metre is the same in both poems.

V. By Marlowe. It appeared in *England's Helicon* with the signature Chr. Marlowe, and two additional stanzas. In *England's Helicon*, 'Love's Answer,' entitled 'The Nymph's reply to the Shepherd,' has five additional stanzas, and is subscribed 'Ignoto.' It was attributed to Sir Walter Raleigh.

VI. By Richard Barnfield. Cf. *Poems: in divers Humors*, and *England's Helicon*.

23. *Pandion*. A king of Athens and father to Philomela. Cf. note on *Lucrece*, 1079.

A LOVER'S COMPLAINT

22, 23. *levell'd . . . intend*. Her eyes were aimed at the sky as a gun on its carriage.

26. *Lend.* See *Notes and Queries*, 1884, Feb. 2, Feb. 16, and March 29.

48, 49. *With sleided . . . secrecy.* Letters were often closed with a piece of silk ribbon the ends of which were placed under the wax-seal of the letter the better to ensure secrecy.

109. *Rounds, bounds, course, stop.* Terms of the *manege* meaning respectively: motion in a circle, leap, race, pause.

111, 112. *Whether . . . steed.* It was impossible to say whether the horse owed the gracefulness of its movements to the skill of the rider, or whether the rider appeared so graceful in his training on account of the horse's docility.

144. *Was my own fee-simple.* I had an absolute power over myself.

153. *Foil.* The setting of a jewel; that which makes it conspicuous. It probably refers here to the thin plate of metal which was (and is still) placed under a valueless stone to give it the appearance of a gem.

157, 158. *Or forc'd . . . way.* 'Or insisted on the examples which tell against her own (apparent) happiness in order to hinder herself from pursuing it by realising the past dangers of others' (Wyndham).

224. *Since . . . me.* I am the altar on which I sacrifice to you, and, therefore, you become my patron or goddess.

229, 230. *What . . . you.* Whatever obeys me on your account works under you since I am your minister.

234. *Which . . . shun.* Who lately avoided the courtship of noble suitors.

235. *Blossoms.* According to Malone, 'the flower of the young nobility.'

241. *Paling . . . receive.* 'Making oneself as it were without form or void' (Wyndham). 'Securing

within the pale of a cloister that heart which had never received the impression of Love' (Malone).

251, 252. *Not to be tempted . . . procur'd.* She sought the cloister in order not to be tempted, but there she only found the liberty to tempt.

APPENDIX A

The Sources and Composition of 'Venus and Adonis'

Adonis, the incestuous son of Myrrha by Theias, King of Assyria (or Cinyras), was so beautiful that the goddess of love became enamoured of him. And all the ancient writers who have related the story, from Panyasis and Apollodorus down to Ovid, agree in making the youth respond to Venus's love. So much so that Zeus having decided that during four months Adonis should be left to himself, the eight remaining months being divided between Persephone and Aphrodite, the boy chose to spend with Aphrodite the months at his own disposal. In Shakespeare's poem, on the contrary, Adonis being courted by Venus is indifferent to the love proffered and even manifests unfeigned repugnance.

Critics generally explain this peculiar treatment of the well-known legend by supposing that Shakespeare combined the narrative of the Adonic fable as told in Ovid's *Metamorphoses* (X, 503-759) with another episode borrowed from the same source, viz., the wooing of Hermaphroditus by the nymph Salmacis (*Met.*, IV, 285-588). But the confusion of the two Ovidian stories had certainly been made, in England, before Shakespeare wrote his *Venus and Adonis*. A certain resistance on the part of Adonis is implied in Spenser's description of the arras of Castle Joyous (*Fairy Queen,* III, i, xxxiv-xxxviii); Adonis's bashfulness is taken for granted by Robert Greene in a 'conceited dittie' sung by Infida in *Never too Late* (1590), which tells of Venus's ineffectual courtship of 'sweet Adon' who dares not 'glaunce his eye' on the goddess. The poem ends as follows:

> Wilt thou let thy Venus die?
>   N'oseres-vous, mon bel amy,
> Adon were unkinde say I,
>   Je vous en prie, pitie me:

.   .   .   .   .

> To let Venus die for woe,
>   N'oseres-vous, mon bel amy,
> That doth love sweete Adon so,
>   Je vous en prie, pitie me.

And Marlowe, in his *Hero and Leander* (12-14), speaks of Adonis's indifference as if it were a well-known thing:

> . . . Venus in her naked glory strove
> To please the careless and disdainful eyes
> Of proud Adonis, that before her lies.

To these instances might be added Constable's 'Shepherd's Song of Venus and Adonis,' if it were not pretty certain that this piece is an imitation of Shakespeare's poem. There must have existed some common source to these English versions of the legend; but this source I have been unable to discover.

It cannot be doubted, however, that Shakespeare was also acquainted with Ovid's treatment of the theme, for several passages in *Venus and Adonis* echo the Latin text (cf. notes on 615-618, 631, 673-678, 883-884, 1115-1116, 1168, and Dürnhöfer, *Venus and Adonis im Verhältnis zu Ovids Metamorphosen*, pp. 35-38). It is no less certain that Shakespeare used Book VIII (ll. 281-297) of the *Metamorphoses* for the description of the Calydonian boar (cf. note on 619-630). The story of Narcissus and Echo (*Met.*, III) may also have provided a hint for the allusion to Narcissus's infatuation with his own person in lines 161, 162, and for Venus's 'wailing note' in lines 829 and following.

On the other hand, Sir Sidney Lee believes that Shakespeare may have been influenced by some of the Italian writers who treated the same subject early in the sixteenth century, such as Lodovico Dolce (*La Favola d' Adone,* 1545), Metello Giovanni Tarchagnota (*L' Adone,* 1550), Girolamo Parabosco (*La Favola d' Adone,* before 1557). 'There are,' he writes, too many details peculiar to Shakespeare's poem and to its Italian predecessors, to preclude the suggestion that Shakespeare was acquainted with the latter and absorbed some of their ornaments and episodes.' But this is, no doubt, crediting Shakespeare with a more intimate knowledge of Italian literature than he probably had. In the same way, Sir Sidney Lee finds that 'in the minute description in Shakespeare's poem of the chase of the hare (673-708), there are curious resemblances to the "Ode de la Chasse" (on a stag hunt) by the French dramatist, Estienne Jodelle, in his *Œuvres et Mélanges Poétiques* (1574).' I must own that I fail to see where the likeness comes in.

More to the point is the comparison which is sometimes made with Lodge's *Scyllas Metamorphosis,* usually called by its running title, *Glaucus and Scylla,* published in 1589. The subject of Lodge's poem is also borrowed from Ovid and it tells of the unrequited love of a woman wooing a reluctant youth. It contains a passage describing Venus's despair at Adonis's death; the metre is the same as the one adopted by Shakespeare, and there are a few resemblances in thought and imagery (cf. notes on 329-336, 589-590). Lodge's poem may have had some influence upon Shakespeare's choice of his subject.

Marlowe's *Hero and Leander* has also been considered as one of Shakespeare's models, and, indeed, echoes of Marlovian thoughts are distinctly heard in a certain number of passages (cf. notes on 3, 263, 264, 720, 751, 768). But none of the similarities recorded is striking enough to be an indisputable proof of the influence of Marlowe on Shakespeare. *Hero and Leander* was licensed for the press on Sept. 28, 1593 —several months after *Venus and Adonis*—and it was not published until 1598. It is not improbable that Shakespeare had read Marlowe's poem in manuscript, but it is impossible to prove that he had.

The metre employed—the six-line stanza rhyming ababcc—is described by Puttenham (*Art of English Poesie,* 1589) as 'most usual,' and it had been in fact adopted by numerous poets, e.g. Gascoigne (*Posies,* 1575), Peele (*Device of the Pageant,* 1585), Nicholas Breton (*The Pilgrimage to Paradise; The Countess of Pembroke's Love,* 1592), Spenser (*Shepherd's Calendar,* 1st Eclogue and part of the 8th Eclogue; *Teares of the Muses; Astrophel*), Lodge (*Scyllas Metamorphosis*). No inference as to the sources can therefore be drawn from Shakespeare's choice of this metre.

Date. In the Dedicatory Letter to Lord Southampton the author speaks of *Venus and Adonis* as 'the first heir of my invention,' and this statement has sometimes been taken as a proof that 'the poem was written or at least designed before Shakespeare undertook any of his dramatic work' (Sidney Lee, *Life,* 142). Some critics have even gone so far as to suppose that the descriptions of the country in *Venus and Adonis* could only have been written while Shakespeare was still in Stratford. But if reminiscences of Shakespeare's rural life are to be found in the poem, echoes of his London life are not absent. The comparison with a dumb play and a chorus (359-360) shows that Shakespeare, as he wrote, was full of his theatrical experience, and lines 508-510 contain an allusion to the plague of 1592-1594. Both the comparison and the allusion are so well embodied in the tale that they render improbable the hypothesis offered by certain scholars that 'the first draught lay in the author's desk through four or five summers, and underwent some retouching before it emerged from the press in its

final shape.' It is safe to admit that *Venus and Adonis*
was written between August, 1592, when the plague
broke out and the theatres were closed, and April 8,
1593, when the poem was entered in the Stationers'
Register. Shakespeare, so far, had only been em-
ployed in revamping old plays and by the words 'the
first heir of my invention' he probably meant that this
narrative poem was his first original work as an author.

Venus and Adonis was published in 1593 by R.
Field, the printer, himself a Stratford man, with the
title-page:

> Venus/and Adonis/
> Vilia miretur vulgus: mihi flauus Apollo
> Pocula Castalia plena ministret aqua.
> [Device]

London/Imprinted by Richard Field, and are to be
sold at/the signe of the white Greyhound in/Paules
Church-yard 1593.[1]

In June, 1594, the book was assigned by Field to
Harrison (Arber, ii, 655), and again, in June, 1596,
to William Leake (Arber, iii, 65), who held the copy-
right until the year 1617. At least seven editions
were printed in Shakespeare's lifetime, and seven post-
humously, viz. 1593, 1594, 1596, 1599 (twice), 1600?,
1602, 1617, 1620, 1627 (Edinburgh), 1630 (twice),
1636, and 1675. For more details, see Sidney Lee's
Introduction to the Oxford facsimile.

---

[1] Compare the title-page of the second edition, repro-
duced as frontispiece of the present volume.

APPENDIX B

The Sources and Publication of 'Lucrece'

The story of Lucrece has been told by numerous writers, the chief versions before Shakespeare's time being those of Dionysius Halicarnassensis (IV, 64, etc.), Diodorus Siculus, Dio Cassius, Ovid (*Fasti,* ii, 721-852), Livy (Bk. I, c. 57-60), Gower (*Confessio Amantis,* Bk. VII), Chaucer (*Legend of Good Women,* 1680-1885), Ser Giovanni Fiorentino (*Il Pecorone,* Giorn. xvi, nov. ii), Bandello (*Novelle,* Pt. ii, nov. xxi), Paynter (*Palace of Pleasure*). Several 'ballets' on the subject had also appeared in 1558, 1560, and 1576.

Shakespeare drew from several of these sources. In Ovid he found certain suggestions—the simile of the wolf and the lamb, for instance,—and a few expressions or ideas (cf. notes on 400, 1604, 1732-1733, 1772-1775). But the number of details common to Shakespeare and Livy, and not to be found in Ovid, is much greater, e.g., Tarquin is brought to his bedroom (120-123); Lucrece confesses to her husband that 'a stranger came and lay' on his pillow; Lucrece's friends assure her that though her body is stained her mind is pure (1655-1656 and 1709-1710); Lucrece asks her friends to swear to avenge her (1689, etc.); Lucrece will not let her example serve as an excuse for light women (1714-1715); Brutus asks his 'wondering friends' to swear to help in revenging Lucrece (1843-1848). What pertains to the change of attitude in Brutus is hardly paralleled by what Ovid says of him. The Argument betrays a knowledge of several historical facts not supplied by Ovid. There are also passages where Shakespeare seems to follow Livy more closely than Ovid (cf. notes on 8-9, 437-439, 477-504).

A few details may have been borrowed from Chaucer. The words 'stalk' and 'dishevelled,' applied respectively to Tarquin and Lucrece, are also in *Legend of Good Women* (1780 and 1830). The statement that Brutus carried the dead body to Rome is neither in Livy nor in Ovid. But in Chaucer Lucrece's self-murder takes place at Rome and her body is carried 'on a bere through al the toun' (1865-1866). For other resemblances see notes on 197-210, 596-630, 1261-1267.

Long ago Malone pointed out resemblances between Daniel's *Complaynt of Rosamonde* and *Lucrece*. The list has since been considerably augmented by Ewig (*Shakespeare's Lucrece*). The most striking similarities are recorded in the notes (cf. 26, 117-119, 492, 556, 1261, 1450-1451, 1660 ff.). It seems pretty certain that Shakespeare learned much of Daniel in technique and that he consciously or unconsciously imitated the tone of the *Complaynt,* especially in Lucrece's piteous accents.

Sir Sidney Lee finds that 'Lucrece's apostrophe to Time (939 ff.) suggests indebtedness to two other English poets, Thomas Watson in *Hecatompathia*, 1582 (xlvii and lxxvii), and Giles Fletcher in *Licia*, 1593 (xxviii).' But such apostrophes were commonplaces in poetry, their ultimate source being traceable to Ovid's *Tristia* (IV. vi. 1-10).

Possibly there is a reminiscence of Virgil in the description of the siege of Troy (cf. note on 1366 ff.).

To sum up: Livy seems to have been the chief source, but Shakespeare used also Ovid and probably Chaucer. For the tone and for a few details he was indebted to contemporary poetry, more particularly to Daniel. But the development of the story is entirely his own.

Metre. There is no reason to suppose that Shakespeare was influenced by any particular poem in the choice of his metre. The seven-line stanza, rhyming ababbcc, or rhyme royal, was perhaps the commonest of all Elizabethan metres. It is thus described by Gascoigne in *Certayne Notes of Instruction,* p. 38 (Arber Reprint): 'Rythme royall is a verse of tenne syllables and seven such verses make a staffe, whereof the first and thirde lines do aunswer (acrosse) in like terminations and rime, the second, fourth, and fifth, do likewise aunswere each other in terminations, and the two last do combine and shut up the sentence: this hath bene called Rithme royall, and surely it is a royall kinde of verse, serving best for graue discourses.' It was used by Chaucer for several of his tales, for his *Compleint unto Pite* and for his *Troylus and Criseyde* (it is sometimes called Troilus verse on that account), and by Spenser for his *Hymns* and his *Ruins of Time*. For the possibility of Shakespeare having first tried the six-line stanza before fixing his choice upon the rhyme royal, see note on 386-395.

Date. *Lucrece* was entered in the Stationers' Register on May 9, 1594 (Arber, ii, 648), under the title of *The Ravyshement of Lucrece,* and was printed in the same year with the following title:

LUCRECE

[Device]

London/Printed by Richard Field, for John Harison, and are/to be sold at the signe of the white Greyhound/in Paules Church-yard. 1594.

This is no doubt the 'graver labour' announced in the Epistle Dedicatory of *Venus and Adonis,* and must have been composed between the spring of 1593 and the spring of 1594. Lucrece was not so popular as *Venus and Adonis,* but it 'pleased the wiser sort,' and no less than four other editions were printed in Shakespeare's lifetime (1598, 1600, 1607, 1616). Three other editions appeared in 1624, 1632, and 1655.

APPENDIX C

'The Phœnix and the Turtle'

In 1601, there appeared a book with the following title:

Loves Martyr/or/Rosalins Complaint./*Allegorically shadowing the truth of Loue*/in the constant Fate of the Phœnix/*and Turtle*./A Poeme interlaced with much varietie and raritie;/*now first translated out of the venerable Italian* Torquato/Caeliano, by Robert Chester./With the true legend of famous King *Arthur*, the last of the nine/Worthies, being the first *Essay* of a new *Brytish* Poet: collected/out of diuerse Authenticall Records./*To these are added some new compositions, of seuerall moderne Writers/whose names are subscribed to their seuerall workes, vpon the/first subject: viz.* the Phœnix *and*/Turtle./*Mar:—Mutare dominum non potest liber notus.*/London/Imprinted for E.B./1601./

The supplementary matter is introduced by a separate title-page:

Hereafter/Follow Diverse/Poeticall Essaies on the former Sub-/iect; viz: the *Turtle* and *Phœnix*./Done by the *best and chiefest of our*/ moderne writers, with their names sub-/scribed to their particular workes:/*neuer before extant.*/And (now first) consecrated by them all generally,/*to the loue and merite of the true-noble Knight*/Sir John Salisburie./*Dignum laude virum Musa vetat mori.*/

[Device]

MDCI.

The author, Robert Chester, apparently was a dependent in the household of the knight to whom the book was dedicated. Sir John Salusbury, a Welsh Gentleman of Lleweni, Denbighshire, was born in December, 1566, or January, 1567. He had in his veins a few drops of royal blood, for his mother, Catherine of Berain, was the granddaughter of Sir Roland Velville, illegitimate son of Henry VII. Sir John married (December, 1586) Ursula Stanley, natural daughter of Henry Stanley, fourth Earl of Derby. He was himself a poet, a patron of letters, and a lover of the drama. He was acquainted with Ben Jonson, and probably with Shakespeare, as has been shown by Sir Israel Gollancz in his article 'Contemporary Lines to Heminges and Condell' (*The Times Literary Supplement,* January 26, 1922). In 1595 he came up to London, frequented the Court and was in great favor with Queen Elizabeth, who appointed him one of her Esquires of the Body (March, 1595). In 1601 he was knighted and it was presumably to celebrate this event that Robert Chester issued his *Loves Martyr.*

Chester's work is a hodge-podge of various poems on unconnected subjects—a history of early England, a description of the nine female worthies, a metrical biography of King Arthur, a prayer, love ditties, an account of the plants, trees, fishes, minerals, beasts, reptiles, insects, and birds found in Paphos, a series of 'Cantoes alphabet-wise,' another series of 'Cantoes verbally written' or posies—more or less cleverly introduced into an allegorical poem, turning upon the marriage of Sir John Salusbury (the Turtle) to Ursula Stanley (the Phœnix), and obscurely relating how the two birds having decided to die on a pyre, 'in a manner sacrificingly,' out of their mystical ashes there arose another Phœnix (Salusbury's first child, Jane).[1]

[1] Dr. Grosart, in his edition of Chester's *Loves Martyr,* confidently advanced the idea that the 'allegory shadowed the love of Q. Elizabeth for the earl of Essex.' It is one of the wildest hypotheses of that ingenious critic. Mr. Carle-

In order to render this homage more valuable, either Robert Chester, or Sir John, or maybe the publisher, asked 'the best and chiefest' among contemporary writers—Shakespeare, John Marston, George Chapman, Ben Jonson, and another person who signed himself 'Ignoto'—to supply a poem on the subject of the Phœnix and Turtle, which poems were collected in the Appendix to *Loves Martyr*.

The contributors did their best to comply with the request and produced a variation on the motive set in *Loves Martyr*. Ignoto insisted upon the denouement which he summed up in the final verse: 'One Phœnix borne, another Phœnix burne.' Marston in his inflated style sang the praises of the 'most exact wondrous creature arising out of the Phœnix and Turtle Doues Ashes.' Chapman chose to marvel at the Turtle's fidelity to his Phœnix, and Ben Jonson celebrated both the constancy of the Turtle and the 'splendor' 'more than mortal' of the Phœnix, who turns out to be a lady full of graces and virtues.

Shakespeare alone of all the contributors does not seem to have clearly understood—and he cannot be blamed—the real meaning of the allegory. He evidently did not discover that the Phœnix and the Turtle were consumed, only in a metaphorical sense, in the flames of their own love, and that they lived again in the person of a beautiful offspring. He made the two birds die 'leaving no posteritie,' and described their obsequies, conducted in the presence of the Eagle, the Swan, and the Crow, as mourners.

This difference in the treatment of the theme is somewhat surprising, and several explanations of it have been offered. Sir Sidney Lee cannot believe that Shakespeare's poem 'was penned for Chester's

ton Brown has discovered a document showing that 'Sir John Salusbury was bitterly opposed to the party of Essex, and therefore was the last person to whom such an allegory as Dr. Grosart constructed would have been dedicated.'

book. It must have been either devised in an idle hour with merely abstract intention, or it was suggested by the death within the poet's own circle of a pair of devoted lovers.' Professor Carleton Brown impressed by 'the frigid and perfunctory tone' of Shakespeare's contribution suggests that the poet's 'relations with Sir John Salusbury were less close than those of Jonson, Marston and Chapman, so that his lines on the Phœnix and Turtle were a matter of courteous compliance rather than a tribute to a personal friend.' Prof. J. Q. Adams supposes that Shakespeare did not trouble 'to read Chester's tedious poem far enough to have unraveled its cryptic meaning,' and he even suspects him of having done his task none too seriously: 'The concluding lines of the Threnos,' adds Prof. Adams, 'may be slyly humorous when the poet calls upon his readers to repair to the urn and

'For these dead birds sigh a prayer.'

Shakespeare certainly was a humorist, but what his real intentions were we shall probably never know.[1]

Sources. A. H. R. Fairchild in his interesting study of the *Phœnix and Turtle* has collected numerous traces of the influence of Chaucer and of the symbolism of the Renaissance emblem writers upon both the conception and the style of Shakespeare's poem. 'It has,' writes Mr. Fairchild, 'a twofold source, stanzas i-v especially being suggested by Chaucer's poem, *The Parlement of Foules,* part IV, 323 to the end, the remaining stanzas (vi-xviii) being adapted to these from the emblem literature and conceptions of Shakespeare's period.' Sir Sidney Lee, on the other hand,

[1] It is hardly worth while to mention A. von Mauntz's laborious interpretation in the volume entitled *Heraldik in diensten der Shakespeare-Forschung* (Berlin, 1903). According to that critic the poem is a complaint over the death of Marlowe and over the loss of his blank verse, the various birds being identified with Spenser, Harvey, Nashe, and Shakespeare.

finds a close affinity with "the imagery of Matthew Roydon's elegy on Sir Philip Sidney, where the turtle-dove and phœnix meet the swan and eagle at the dead hero's funeral and there play rôles somewhat similar to those which Shakespeare assigns the birds in his 'poetical essaie.'" Some of the resemblances with Chaucer's *Parlement of Foules* are striking enough and they are recorded in the notes. But I wonder whether it is necessary to find any particular source at all for Shakespeare's use of the different emblems of the allegory, for they were part of the symbolical language of the time.

Metre. The *Phœnix and Turtle* consists of thirteen quatrains in truncated trochaics rhyming abba. The concluding Threnos consists of five three-line stanzas, in octosyllabic trochaics, each stanza having a single rhyme.

APPENDIX D

The Publication and Authorship of 'The Passionate Pilgrim'

In 1599 William Jaggard issued a poetical miscellany under the title of

THE/Passionate/Pilgrime./By W. Shakespeare./
[Device]
At London/Printed for W. Jaggard, and are/to be sold by W. Leake, at the Grey-/hound in Paules Churchyard./1599.

The volume contained twenty lyrical pieces, the last six of which were preceded by a second title-page running thus:

Sonnets/to sundry notes of Musicke./
[Device]
At London/Printed for W. Jaggard, and are/to be sold by W. Leake, at the Grey-/hound in Paules Churchyard/1599.

Out of the twenty poems only five are indisputably by Shakespeare. These are numbers I, II, III, V of *The Passionate Pilgrim* and II of *Sonnets to Sundry Notes,* which are extracted from Shakespeare's Sonnets (Nos. 138 and 144) and from *Love's Labour's Lost* (IV. iii. 60-73; IV. ii. 110-123; IV. iii. 101-120). Four other poems, IV, VI, IX, XI, are on the subject of Venus and Adonis. No XI appeared in 1596 in Bartholomew Griffin's *Fidessa,* and there is no reason to doubt that the sonnet was actually written by the poet to whom it was ascribed. As regards IV, VI, IX, critics are divided. Malone thought that they must be 'essays of the author when he first conceived the notion of writing a poem on the subject of *Venus and*

Adonis,' and that 'these little pieces bear the strongest
mark of the hand of Shakespeare.' Dowden, likewise,
was of opinion that 'nothing in any one of these son-
nets forbids the idea of Shakespeare's authorship.' He
pointed out that IV and VI recall a passage in *The
Taming of the Shrew* (Induction, ii. 51-53) and that
the words 'brakes' and 'queen of love' appear in IX as
well as in *Venus and Adonis.* But as I have shown
in note to VI the details of the picture in *The Taming
of the Shrew* and in *The Passionate Pilgrim* are dif-
ferent; and the repetition of such ordinary expressions
as 'queen of love' and 'brakes' does not prove much.
These resemblances might just as well be reminis-
cences of *Venus and Adonis,* as is suggested by Sir
Sidney Lee, who refuses to see there any trace of
Shakespeare's workmanship. It should also be noted
that IV, VI, and IX are remarkable for their lack of
imagery: they scarcely contain any simile and meta-
phor. The man who wrote them was singularly de-
void of imagination, a thing which cannot be said of
Shakespeare but which is certainly true of Griffin, as
XI and the whole of *Fidessa* demonstrates. It is most
probable that the four Venus-Adonis sonnets come
from the same hand, that of Bartholomew Griffin.

The other poems in the book—with the exception of
VII, X, XIII, XIV, and I, III, IV of *Sonnets to
Sundry Notes,* which have nothing Shakespearean
about them—have been restored to their owners (cf.
notes).

The Passionate Pilgrim met with success. As may
be inferred from the title-page of the 1612 edition, a
second edition was called for, of which no copy is
known to exist. In 1612 Jaggard issued another
edition with the following title:

The / Passionate / Pilgrime / or / *Certaine Amorous
Sonnets* / betweene Venus *and* Adonis / *newly corrected
and aug-/mented/By W. Shakespere*/The third Edi-

tion./Whereunto is newly ad/ded two Love-Epistles,
the first/from *Paris* to *Hellen*, and *Hellens* answere
backe/againe to *Paris*/Printed for W. Jaggard./1612.

The two additions announced on the title-page were
extracted from Heywood's *Troia Britannica*, a collec-
tion which Jaggard himself had published in 1609.
This piece of unscrupulous effrontery elicited a pro-
test from Heywood which appeared as a postscript to
his *Apology for Actors* (1612): "Here likewise I must
necessarily insert a manifest injury done to me in that
worke by taking the two Epistles of Paris to Helen,
and Helen to Paris, and printing them in a lesse vol-
ume, under the name of another, which may put the
world in an opinion I might steale them from him,
and hee to doe himselfe right, hath since published
them in his owne name: but as I must acknowledge my
lines not worthy his [i.e. Shakespere's] patronage
under whom he [i.e. Jaggard] hath published them,
so the Author [i.e. Shakespere] I know much of-
fended with M. Jaggard that (altogether unknowne
to him) presumed to make so bold with his name."
This formal statement proved effective, for Jaggard
cancelled the fallacious title-page and issued the re-
maining copies with a new one from which he omitted
Shakespeare's name.

APPENDIX E

The Authorship of 'A Lover's Complaint'

When Thorpe published Shakespeare's *Sonnets* in 1609 he appended a poem in forty-nine seven-line stanzas, entitled *A Lover's Complaint*, which he gave out as written by William Shakespeare. The metre used is that of *Lucrece*, and it is true that several passages exhibit a felicity of phrase which reminds one of Shakespeare's characteristic sweetness. Yet it is to be doubted whether Thorpe was justified in attributing *A Lover's Complaint* to the author of the *Sonnets*. We know that Elizabethan publishers were not very scrupulous in their ascriptions and the methodical analysis of the poem made by Prof. J. W. Mackail (in *Essays and Studies* by members of the English Association, 1912) seems to prove that Shakespeare could not have written that pathetic but somewhat affected lamentation. The poem contains an unusually high proportion of words not to be found in Shakespeare's authentic work, together with a great number of Latinisms and other syntactical peculiarities. It may be added that the rhythm of many lines is too awkward to have satisfied Shakespeare's subtle ear even in the period of his apprenticeship. For my part, I very strongly question the authenticity of this piece.

APPENDIX F

The Text of the Present Edition

The text of the present volume is based, by permission of the Oxford University Press, upon that of the Oxford Shakespeare, edited by W. J. Craig, except for the following changes:

1. Punctuation and spelling have been normalized to accord with modern English practice, e.g. forgo (forego), warlike (war-like).

2. Characteristic old forms (e.g., murther, Troyan) and euphonic abbreviations (e.g. th'annexions) are retained.

3. The following alterations in Craig's text have been made, all in conformity with the readings of the First Quartos. The readings of the present edition precede the colon, while Craig's readings follow it.

VENUS AND ADONIS

188	gone?: gone;
317	was: is
484	earth: world
591	cheek: cheeks
601	so: as
896	all: sore
962	eye: eyes
1134	thou: you

LUCRECE

135	That: For
217	stroken: strucken
319	needle: neeld
584	look'st: look'dst
772	cureless: curseless

812   cote: quote
1029   foul defiled: foul-defiled
1145   not: nor
1338   villain: villein
1352   her: their
1544   to beguild: so beguil'd
1615   woes: woe

PASSIONATE PILGRIM

XI. 14.   run: ran
XIV. 8   scorn or: scorn of   conster: construe

SONNETS TO SUNDRY NOTES OF MUSIC

IV. 51   round me on th'ear: ring my ear

LOVER'S COMPLAINT

41   lets: let
47   moe: more
198   pallid: paled

APPENDIX G

Suggestions for Collateral Reading

E. Dowden: *Shakespeare. A critical study of his Mind and Art,* 12th ed., 1901, pp. 49-52.

F. S. Boas: *Shakespeare and his Predecessors,* 1896, pp. 158-163.

R. M. Alden: *Shakespeare,* 1922, pp. 105-117.

Sir Sidney Lee: *Life of Shakespeare,* new ed., 1922, pp. 141-150; 160; 267-273.

J. Q. Adams: *Life of Shakespeare,* 1923, pp. 145-160.

J. P. Reardon: 'Shakespeare's Venus and Adonis and Lodge's Scilla's Metamorphosis.' (Shakespeare Society Papers, iii, 1847, 143-146.)

M. Dürnhöfer: *Shakesperes 'Venus and Adonis' im Verhältnis zu Ovids Metamorphosen und Constables Schäfergesang.* Halle, 1890 (Diss.).

T. Sarrazin: *William Shakespeares Lehrjahre.* (Litterar-historische Forschungen, v), Weimar, 1897.

W. Ewig: *Shakespeares Lucrece. Eine litterar-historische Untersuchung.* Kiel, 1899 (Diss.). Also in *Anglia,* xxii.

Robert Chester's *Loves Martyr,* edited with Introduction, etc., by the Rev. Alexander B. Grosart. New Shakespeare Society, 1878.

A. H. R. Fairchild: 'The Phœnix and Turtle: a critical and historical interpretation.' (*Englische Studien,* xxxiii, pp. 337 sqq.), 1904.

Poems by Sir John Salusbury and Robert Chester. With an Introduction by Carleton Brown. (Bryn Mawr College Monographs, xiv), 1913.

A. Höhnen: *Shakespeares Passionate Pilgrim,* Jena, 1867 (Diss.).

E. Dowden: Introduction to Griggs's facsimile of *The Passionate Pilgrim*, 1883.

E. P. Kuhl: 'Shakespeare and the Passionate Pilgrim.' (*Modern Language Notes*, xxxiv, p. 313), 1919.

J. W. Mackail: 'A Lover's Complaint.' (*Essays and Studies* by members of the English Association, iii, 51-70), 1912.

J. M. Robertson: *Shakespeare and Chapman. A thesis of Chapman's authorship of A Lover's Complaint, etc.*, 1917.

The best editions of the Poems are those in the 'Arden Shakespeare,' by C. Knox Pooler, 1911; in the 'Tudor Shakespeare,' by C. Brown, 1913. Other valuable editions are: *The Poems of Shakespeare*, edited by George Wyndham, 1898; the facsimile reprints of *Venus and Adonis, Rape of Lucrece* and *Passionate Pilgrim*, edited with Introduction and Bibliography by Sidney Lee, Oxford, 1905; *Venus and Adonis and Rape of Lucrece*, edited by C. H. Herford (Eversley Shakespeare), 1900,

INDEX OF WORDS GLOSSED

(Figures in full-faced type refer to page numbers. Ven = *Venus and Adonis*, Luc = *The Rape of Lucrece*, Phœ = *The Phœnix and the Turtle*, Pas = *The Passionate Pilgrim*, Son = *Sonnets to Sundry Notes of Music*, Lov = *A Lover's Complaint*.)